Black and White

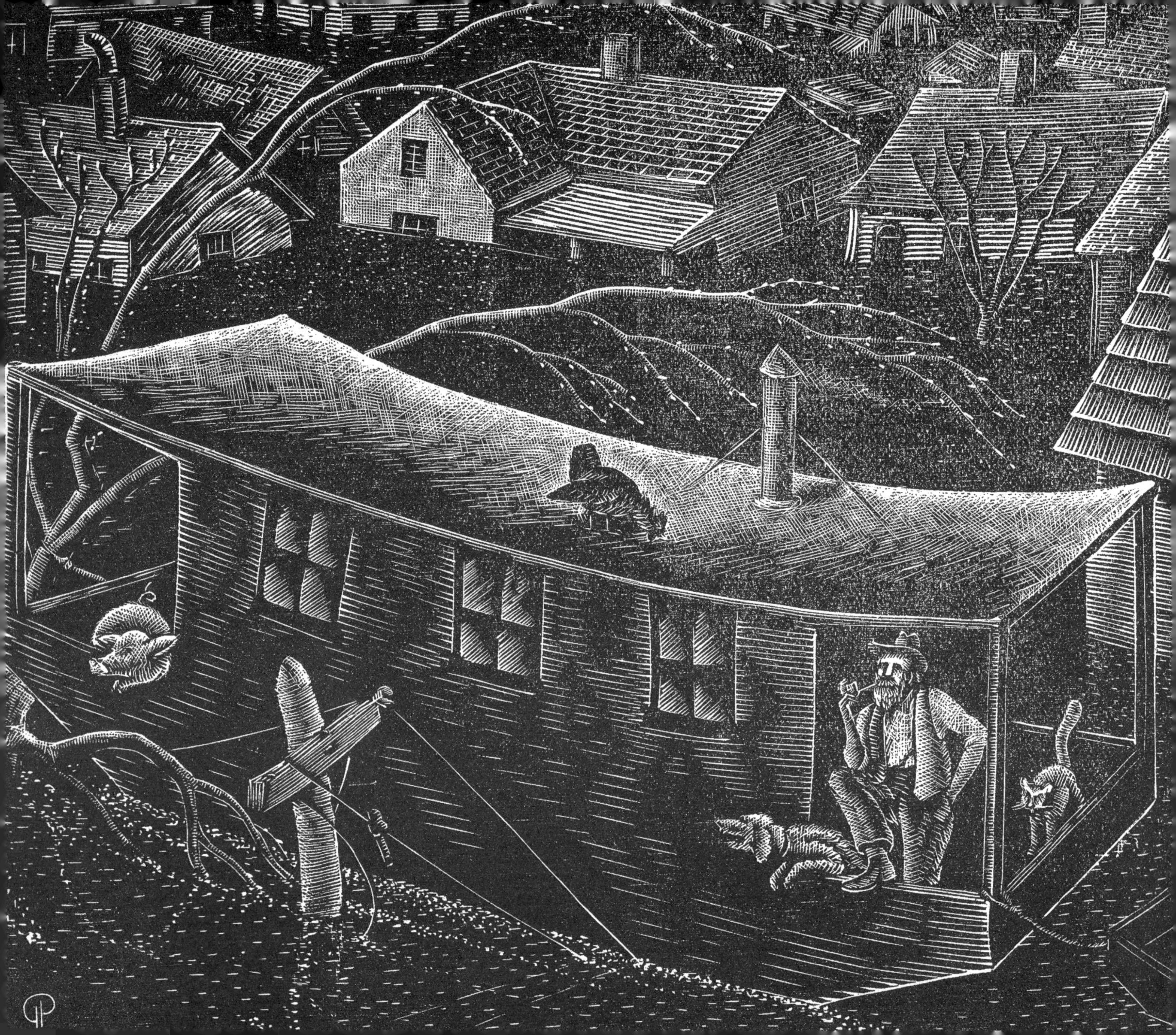

Black and White

Kentucky Prints and Printmakers
from the Collection of Warren and Julie Payne

PFA Press
Louisville, Kentucky
2020

All the prints in this book are from the collection of Warren and Julie Payne.

Published by PFA Press
Louisville, Kentucky 40207
www.paynefinearts.com

Printed in Canada by Friesens

Library of Congress Control Number: 2020903187

ISBN: 978-0-578-65145-3

Front cover: *Pioneer Woman* by Wallace Kelly

Frontispiece: *Noah* by Grover Page

Artist biographies: Warren Payne

Photography and design: Julie Payne

Contents

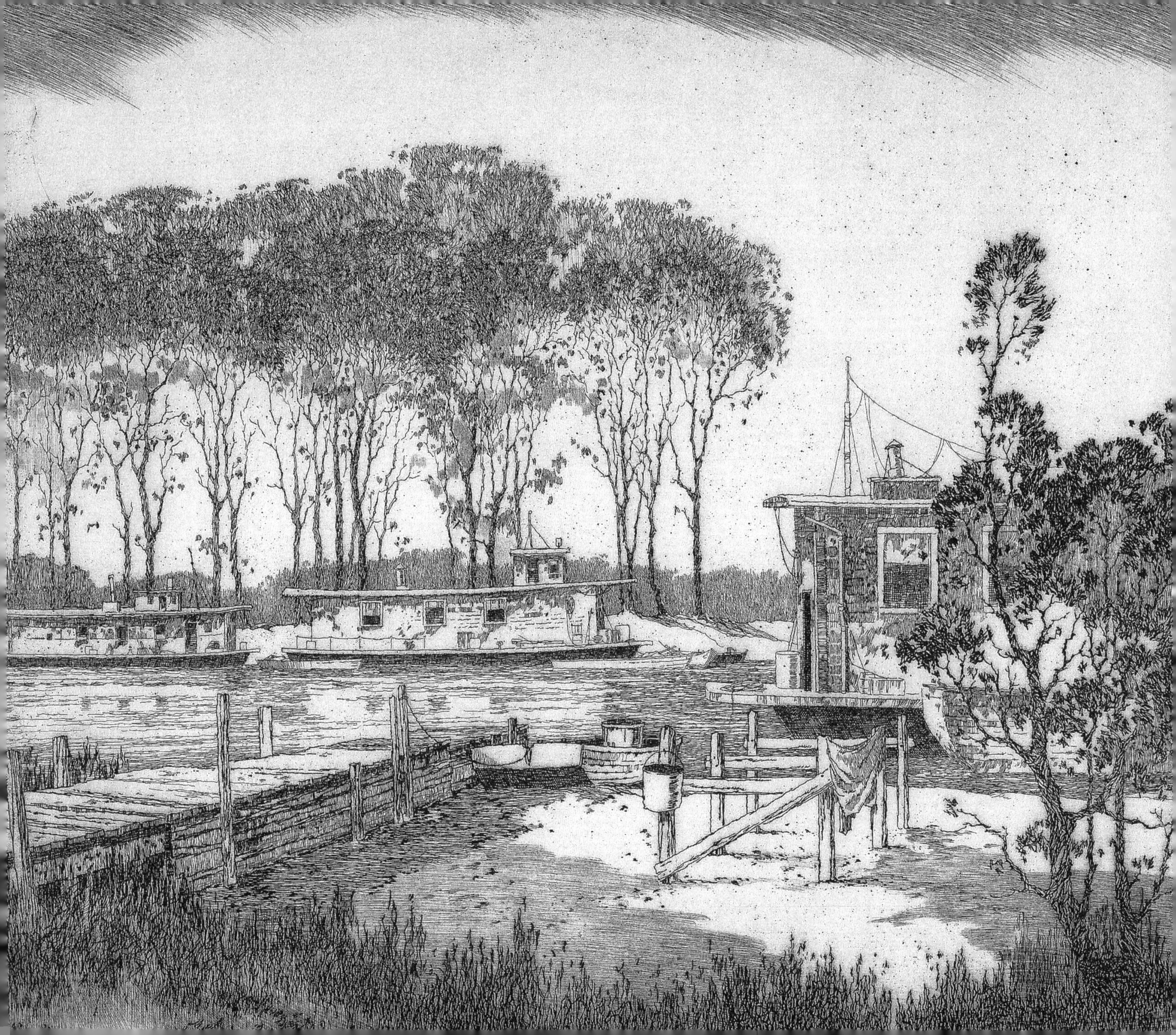

Introduction

IN 1992 LIBRARIAN MARTIN F. SCHMIDT brought out his *Kentucky Illustrated: The First Hundred Years* (University Press of Kentucky). His volume "of early views of Kentucky" remains *the* resource for images of the sites and goings-on in the Commonwealth through its first century. "Illustrations played an important role in shaping the Kentucky image, both internal and external," Schmidt notes in his introduction.

On the whole, those original images, published in 19th century newspapers, journals and histories, were produced by yeoman illustrators, engravers and printers, but not by fine artists producing wholly original works of art. The point was to show, e.g., a city, a factory, a natural occurrence, the image having value more as journalism than art.

Yes, during the American Scene era of the 1930s, broadly referred to as the WPA era, artists produced images of historic sites and personages in a conscious effort to celebrate the history of the country and its people. Sometimes the images were intended to criticize and question the status quo. But in all cases the works reflected the artist, his training, his thinking, his technique and more. They were not topographical illustrations, and, as we see, occasionally reveal artistic license.
Some of the early works in this book were produced by those yeoman engravers. However, they were reproducing original works by professional artists. The distinction is important. The painter-etchers of the late 19th century made prints of their and others' paintings. These prints – reproductives – were original works of art and are treated as such. So, too, are the engravings of drawings and paintings by our early artists.

C. Winston Haberer

Along Towhead Island

etching

edition 19/100

8 x 9 3/4 inches

It's important that the reader know why this book is the way it is. To make the cut, first and foremost, the prints had to be in our collection.

Secondly, the prints had to be black and white. This reflects my love for black and white – in movies, interior design, photography, you name it. When I began my journalistic career at the *Courier-Journal* in Louisville, Kentucky, newspapers were black and white, and they were produced through a relief process called letterpress. Letterpress is enjoying a revival among creative printers.

Thirdly, the artist or the image had to be tied to Kentucky. One Kentucky-born woman was one of the early members of the St. Augustine, Florida, artist colony. So her contribution is a scene of old St. Augustine. One artist was born in Pennsylvania, lived in Nashville, Tennessee, and is represented by a block print of Mount Rainier in Washington state – but she was an important teacher in Bowling Green, Kentucky. And nationally known artists were compelled to produce images of Abraham Lincoln's birthplace, and others, of Federal Hill, My Old Kentucky Home.

A number of the prints are river scenes, some by Ohio artists, but the river is the Ohio, and the Ohio is mostly Kentucky's. There are shanty-boat prints, too, reflecting an interest I've had for years that resulted in the 2019 *Shantyboat Life on the Ohio* exhibition at the Filson Historical Society in Louisville. Artists came to Kentucky to capture that riparian way of life from the 1920s through the 1940s. Many of the Cincinnati depictions are from the "Kentucky side."

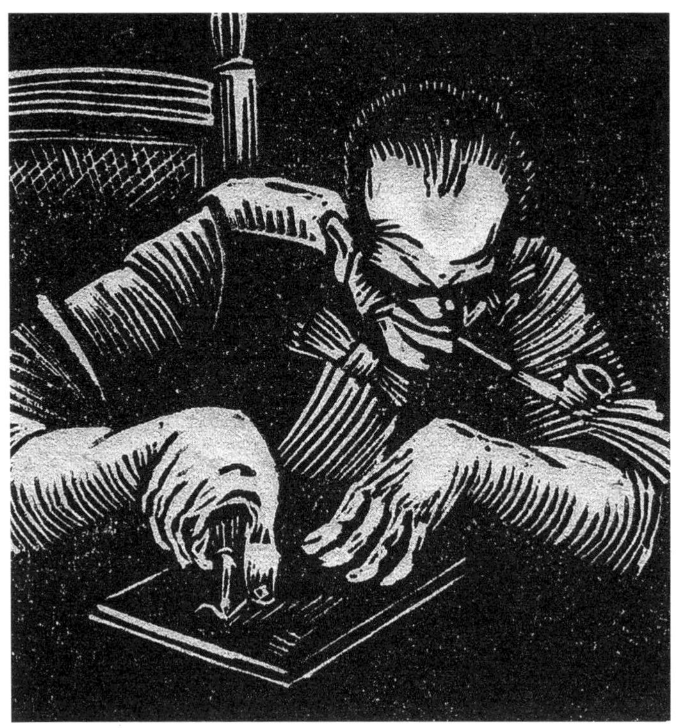

Grover Page, *Self-portrait*, block print, 2 3/4 x 2 5/8 inches

The reader also needs to know that the book is arranged chronologically, starting in 1828 and ending in 2004 for the John Wezley Haywood print. That way, e.g., the American Regionalists are grouped together, and the reader can see a progression in style and subject matter.

Many of the regional artists in the book will be completely unknown to most readers. Many of them studied with some of the greatest artists in American history. Some of their prints were beautiful and great, and some were not. But they were part of a larger group, all working toward some goal in their hearts. They can't be forgotten; they won't be ignored.

—Warren Payne, Louisville, Kentucky

PROCESSES

Printmaking can be a matter of innies and outies. In one method, the image is formed by lines incised in a metal plate. In another, the image is formed by what's sticking out from a block of wood. Here are the three basic processes.

Intaglio: The images produced are called etchings and engravings, the latter also referred to as drypoint. The images are made by lines cut into a metal plate, usually copper or steel. In etching the lines are enhanced by having acid eat into them, a chemical process capable of great subtlety. In drypoint the lines are enhanced by the amount of pressure used to make the lines. Different tools are used in each. In both the plate is inked and run through a press. More subtlety can be achieved by how the ink is used.

Relief: The images produced are called block prints. The images are made from what remains after the artist cuts away what he doesn't want to show. The oldest is the woodcut. Wood is cut away to leave the wanted image. While an intaglio line is below the surface of the plate, the woodcut line is raised above the block. Another relief process is the wood engraving. This is formed from the end grain of the wood block and is also capable of great subtlety. In both the block is inked and run through a press. Block prints are also made using linoleum.

Planographic: This process is neither an innie nor an outie. The image is produced by drawing on a lithographic stone, so it sits on the surface. The drawing is done with a greasy crayon, the stone moistened and a greasy ink used. The moistened part repels the grease and doesn't appear. Only the greasy drawing is reproduced after being run through the press.

M.H.Jouett, del.

MATTHEW HARRIS JOUETT's talent, winning personality, strong character and tragic early death cemented his almost-legendary reputation as Kentucky's first, great, native-born painter.

Jouett (1787-1827) trained with celebrated portraitist Gilbert Stuart in Boston, Massachusetts, and made his career as a portrait painter in Kentucky and up and down the Ohio and Mississippi rivers. He inspired a generation of painters, and his portraits "provide a progressive pageant of the Kentucky story," journalist E.A. Jonas wrote in *Matthew Harris Jouett Kentucky Portrait Painter 1787-1827* (J.B. Speed Memorial Museum).

Among those portraits were likenesses of the Rev. Horace Holley, president of Transylvania University in Lexington from 1818 to 1827, and his wife, Mary Austin Holley. Jouett, who had attended Transylvania while a young man, was close with the Holleys and in 1827 gave Holley a drawing of the main building at Transylvania. When Holley died that same year, his widow wanted the Jouett drawing included in a book memorializing her husband. Charles Caldwell, a physician who taught at Transylvania, brought out A *Discourse on the Genius and Character of the Rev. Horace Holley, LL. D., Late President of Transylvania University* in 1828 with an engraving of the Jouett drawing by E.G. Gridley.

Gridley is usually described as being from Cincinnati, Ohio. And an E.G. Gridley appears in the *Cincinnati Directory* in 1818 and 1825 as an engraver and copper-plate printer. One of the citations includes "Massachusetts" after Gridley's name before giving the engraver's Cincinnati address. There is also a listed engraver named Enoch G. Gridley, who was active from 1803 to 1818 in Philadelphia, Pennsylvania, New York City and Boston. Caldwell's book was published in Boston. Known Enoch G. Gridley prints are signed E.G. Gridley, as is the Jouett engraving.

Jouett's portrayal of the 1818 Transylvania building constitutes his only known print. The engraving was published a year after the artist's death, and the building depicted burned to the ground a year later.

The Principal Building of Transylvania University, inscribed to President Holley
copper-plate engraving
1828
4 x 6 1/8 inches

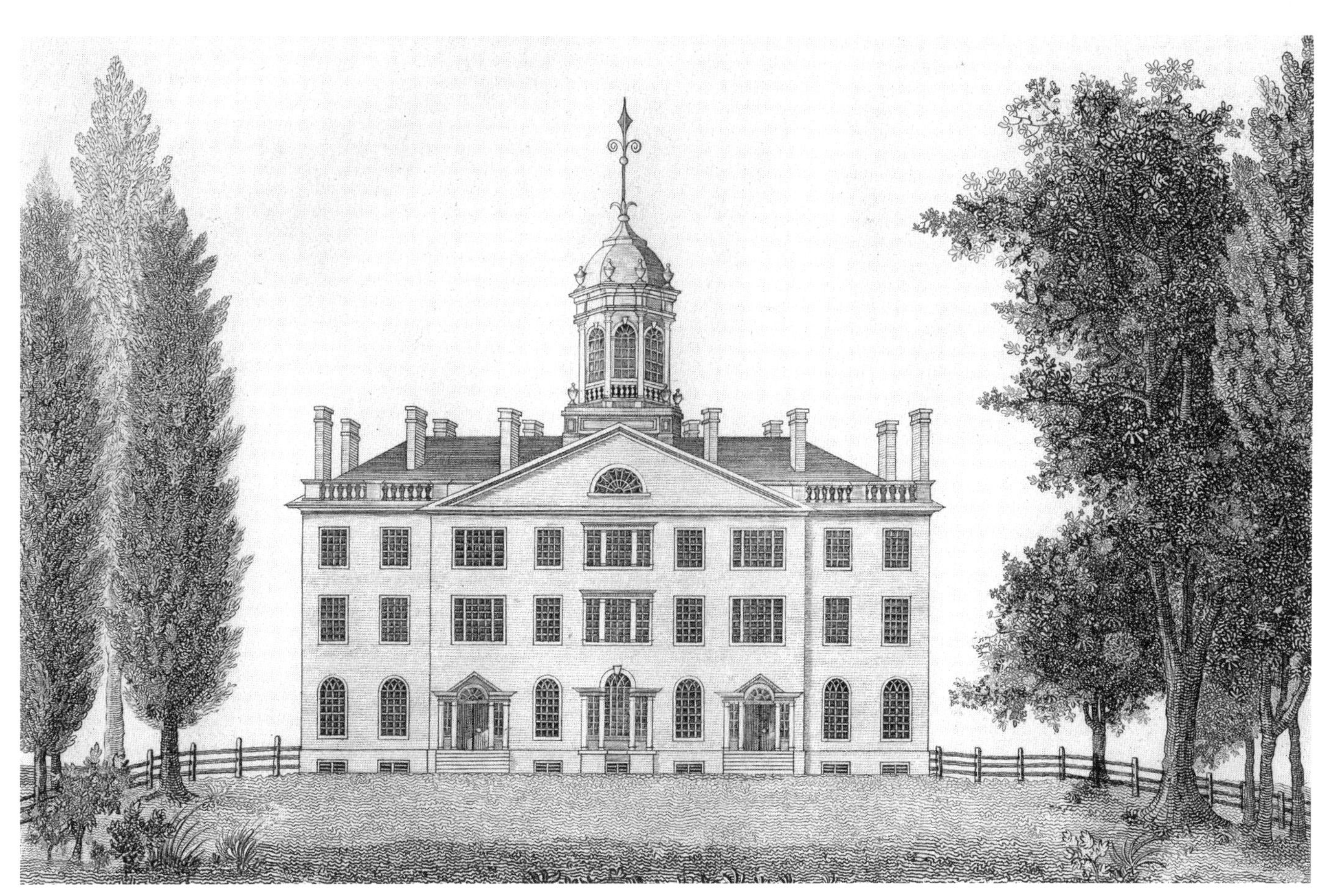

W. Ranney

In 1850 the American Art-Union displayed **WILLIAM TYLEE RANNEY**'s painting *Daniel Boone's First View of Kentucky* in its New York City gallery. As was the AAU's wont, an etched version of the painting was published, and it served as the frontispiece of the May 1850 *Bulletin of the American Art Union*.

The artist, Ranney (1813-1857), was known for his history paintings and his love of scenes from the South and West. He was born in Connecticut, raised in North Carolina and worked in New York City. It is interesting to note that two years after the Art-Union exhibited *Boone's First View*, Ranney produced *Squire Boone Crossing the Mountains with Stores for his Brother Daniel, Encamped in the Wilds of Kentucky*. And it is also interesting to note that Ranney painted a view of Boone leading settlers through the Cumberland Gap, *Boone's Party*, that resides at the Duncan Tavern Historic Center in Paris, Kentucky.

The Art-Union was founded to promote American art, to support our artists and to develop an audience for their art. An AAU membership cost $5 a year and brought the subscriber an engraving of a contemporary painting in the AAU collection. The New-York Historical Society guide to its Art-Union collection notes that "most of the artwork purchased and engraved for distribution by the AAU was historical in subject, as was the fashion of the day." A number of the prints, such as that of George Caleb Bingham's painting *The Jolly Flat Boat Men*, have become highly collectible.

The etcher of *Boone's First View*, Alfred Jones (1819-1900), was born in England and came to the United States in the first half of the 19th century. In 1839 he was in New York City studying at the National Academy of Design; he became an academician in 1851. By the end of the Civil War, he was the president of the United States Bank Note Co. of New York.

Daniel Boone's first view of Kentucky
etching
1850
5 1/2 x 7 7/8 inches

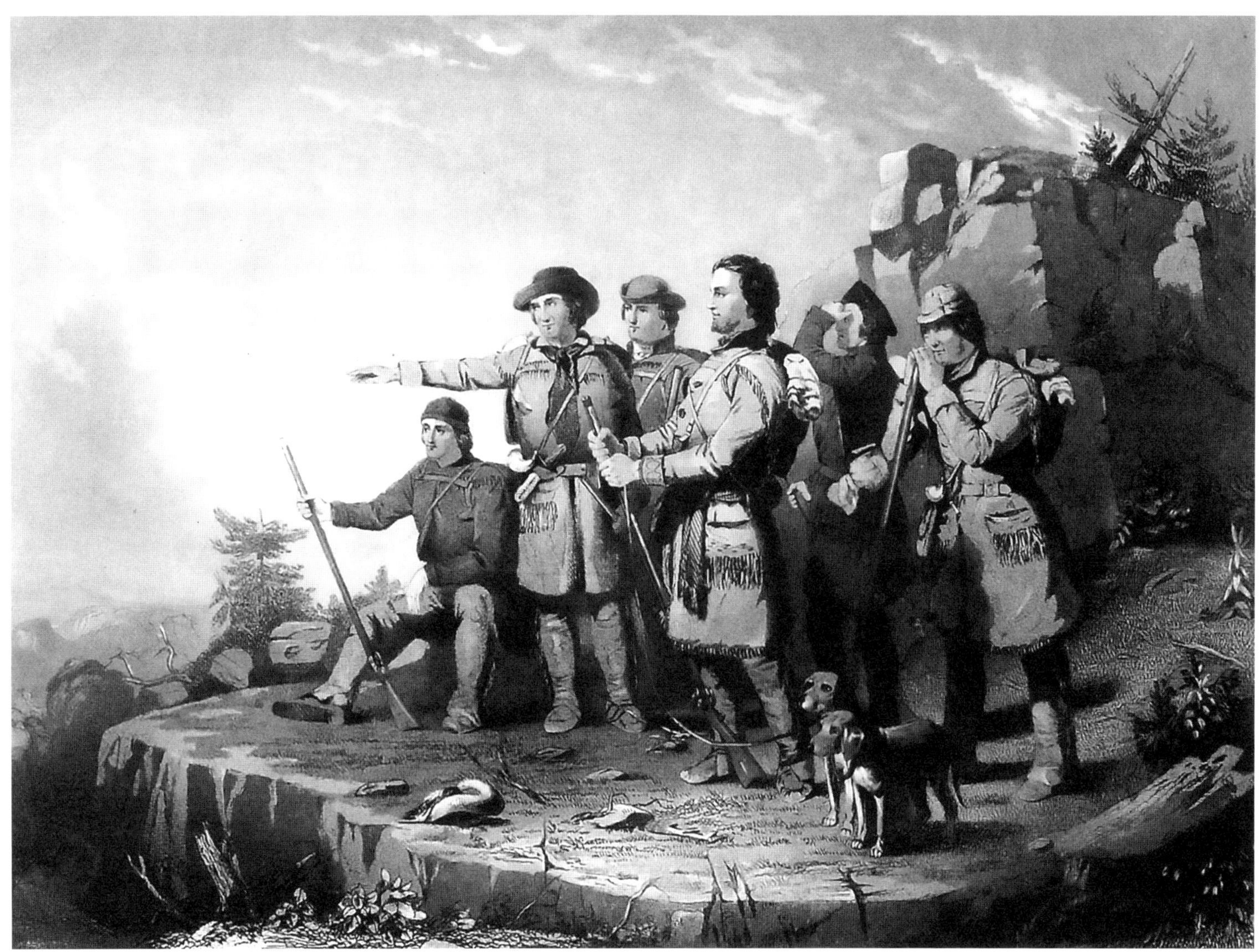

E. Troye

EDWARD TROYE, "the Painter of Thoroughbred Stories," as Genevieve Baird Lacer's popular book rightly deemed him, was born in Switzerland and came to the United States in 1831. He first exhibited in Philadelphia at the Pennsylvania Academy of the Fine Arts, attracting the attention of the racing aristocracy. He proceeded to become the foremost mid-19th century painter of horses in America.

Troye (1808-1874) painted horse portraits in New York, Virginia, South Carolina, Louisiana, Tennessee and Kentucky. He spent a number of years in Kentucky, living in Lexington and in Georgetown, where he is buried.

His paintings were reproduced in the country's first magazine of sport, *The American Turf Register and Sporting Magazine.* Engravings after Troye paintings served as frontispieces for the periodical. These prints were executed by some of the best American engravers.

The print opposite, *Black Maria*, is a steel engraving by Capewell & Kimmel of Troye's 1834 painting *Commodore John Cox Stevens' Black Maria Held by Bill Patrick*. It appeared in *Frank Forester's Horse and Horsemanship of the United States and British Provinces of North America* of 1857. There is a larger version engraved by A.L. Dick for the New York newspaper *The Spirit of the Times; A Chronicle of the Turf, Field Sports, Literature and the Stage* in 1839.

Black Maria
copper-plate engraving
1857
4 1/8 x 6 inches

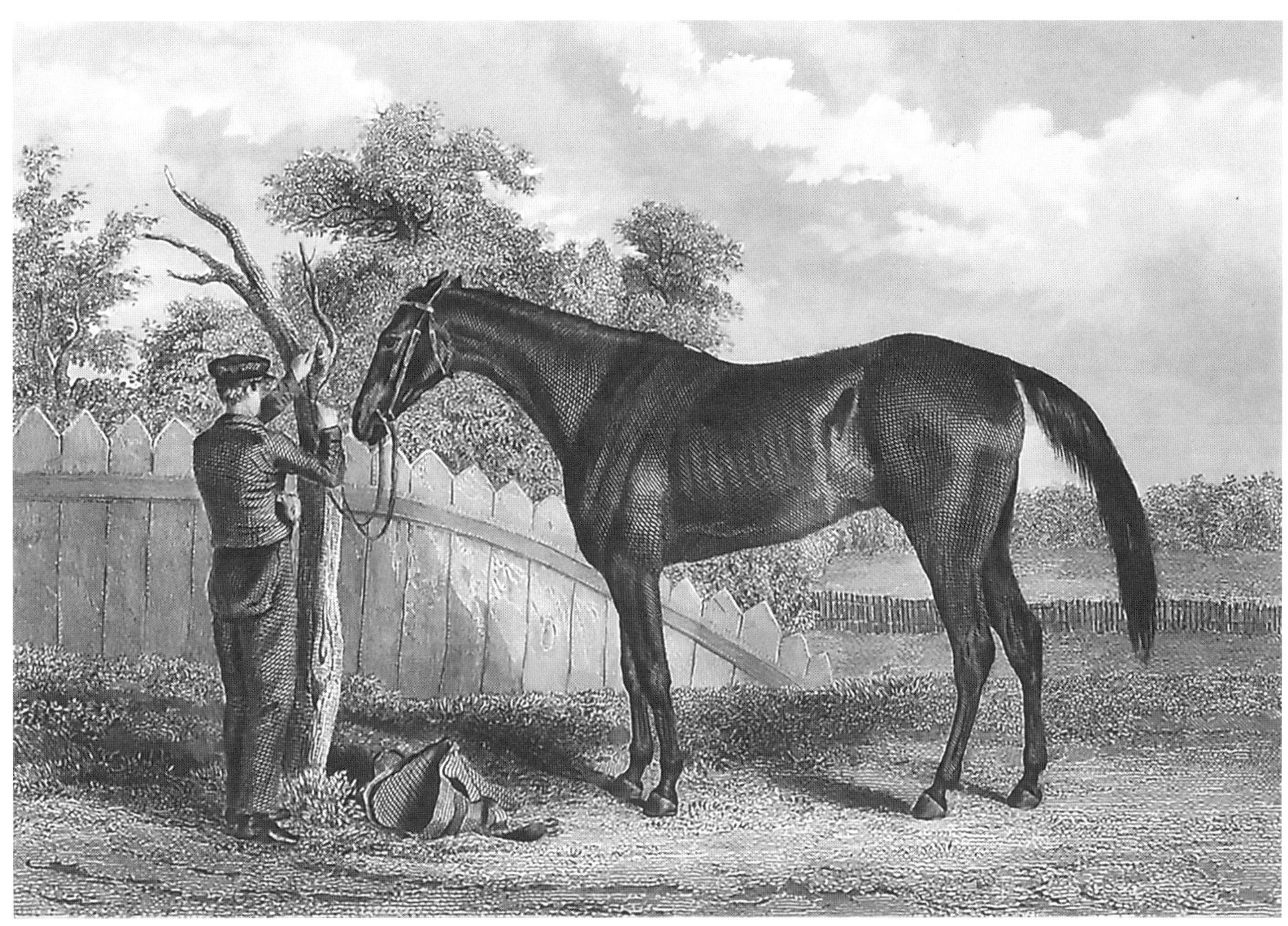

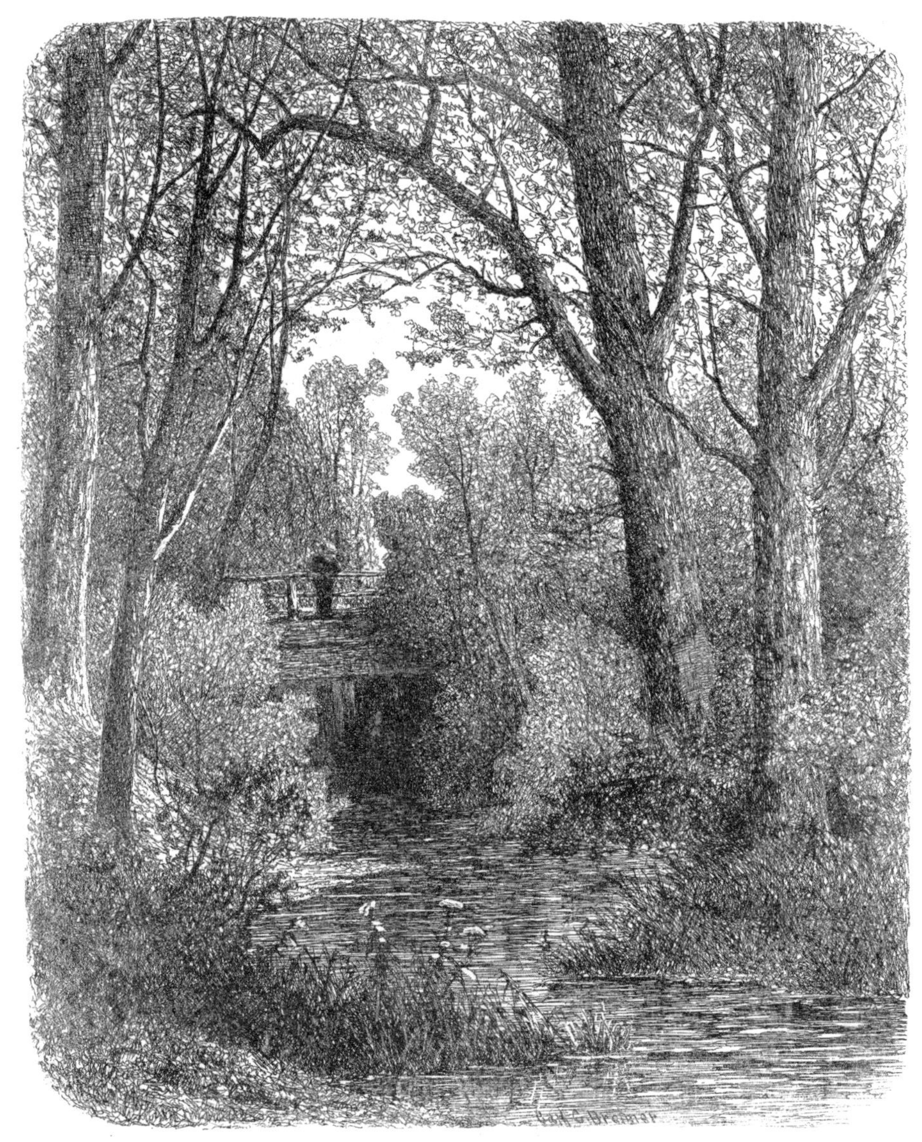

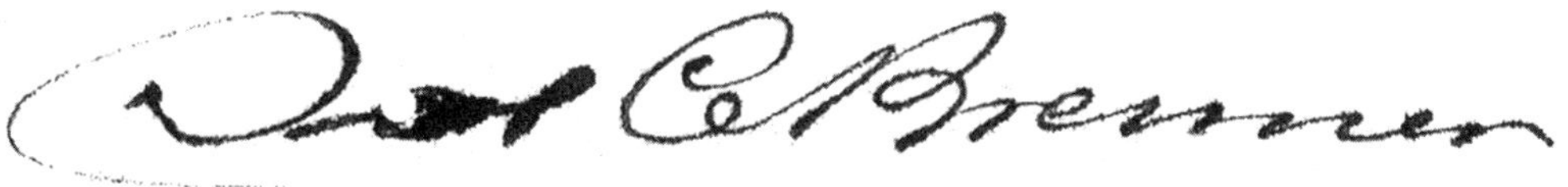

CARL CHRISTIAN BRENNER is considered Kentucky's first professional landscape painter, working from the early 1870s until his death in 1888 at the age of 49. Unlike the watercolorists of the early 19th century, Brenner didn't paint to depict particular sites but, simply, to paint.

The Brook
etching
5 3/4 x 4 3/4 inches

Brenner (1838-1888) was a native of Germany, where he received some art training, and came to America when he was 15. His family settled in Louisville, which had a burgeoning population of German Roman Catholics. Brenner's artistic desires were subdued under family pressure, and he established a paint store and painted signs. When that family pressure dissolved, Brenner turned his attention to landscape painting and in 1874 sold an important oil to the Corcoran Gallery of Art in Washington, D.C. His career took off, and he painted scenes throughout the Commonwealth and in Northeastern and Western America.

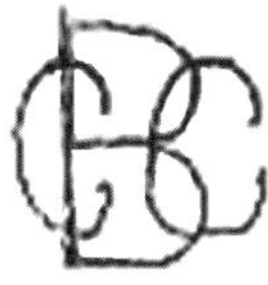

Brenner was aware of the etching revival that had been going on in France and England for decades and became popular in the United States in the 1870s and 1880s. He took to the needle and produced a series of etchings with such titles as *The Crossing Log; Mill Dam, Silver Creek; Cottage by the Hillside* (a reproductive of one of his paintings); *Fishing;* and *Laurel Creek.* A catalog from the Louisville Industrial Exposition of 1879-1880 shows that Brenner displayed 15 etchings for sale. The Corcoran was a willing buyer, acquiring a grouping. According to family information, Brenner's etching period began and ended in the 1870s, when he decided to concentrate on painting.

Small groups of the etchings showed up alongside his paintings in Speed Art Museum exhibitions in the 20th century, and in 1956 the Hite Art Institute at the University of Louisville had an exhibition of a dozen etchings.

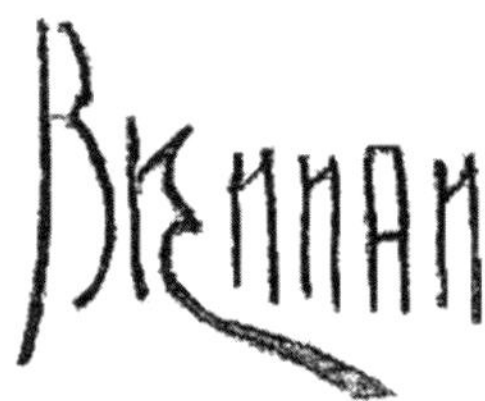

Louisville, Kentucky, native **ALFRED LAURENS BRENNAN** (1853-1921) was considered one of the finest pen-and-ink illustrators of the 1880s and 1890s. His *New-York Tribune* obituary reported that he had "contributed more than 10,000 drawings to various American publications."

Brennan trained in Cincinnati, Ohio, where the family moved after the Civil War, studying with such luminaries as H.F. Farny and Frank Duveneck. By 1879 Brennan had established a studio in New York City. He was described as "the finest technician in America" by no less a colleague than etcher, lithographer and writer Joseph Pennell.

Brennan's fine-art output included watercolors, oil paintings and etchings. His *Divination in Tea-Leaves* was published in S.R. Koehler's *American Art Review* in 1879. Koehler, in his accompanying critique, wrote that Brennan executed other prints but didn't think much of them. However, "he intends … to continue to ply the needle."

Divination in Tea-Leaves shows the detail for which Brennan was famous. Behind the seated figure is a tiled fireplace surround. The tiles show a whirling figure and bear the name *Vivien*. The Minton China Works in England brought out a set of tiles inspired by Alfred Tennyson's *Idylls of the King* around 1876. Vivien, of the "lissome limbs," is a seductress in the Arthurian poetry cycle.

Divination in Tea-Leaves
etching
1879
8 1/4 x 5 7/8 inches

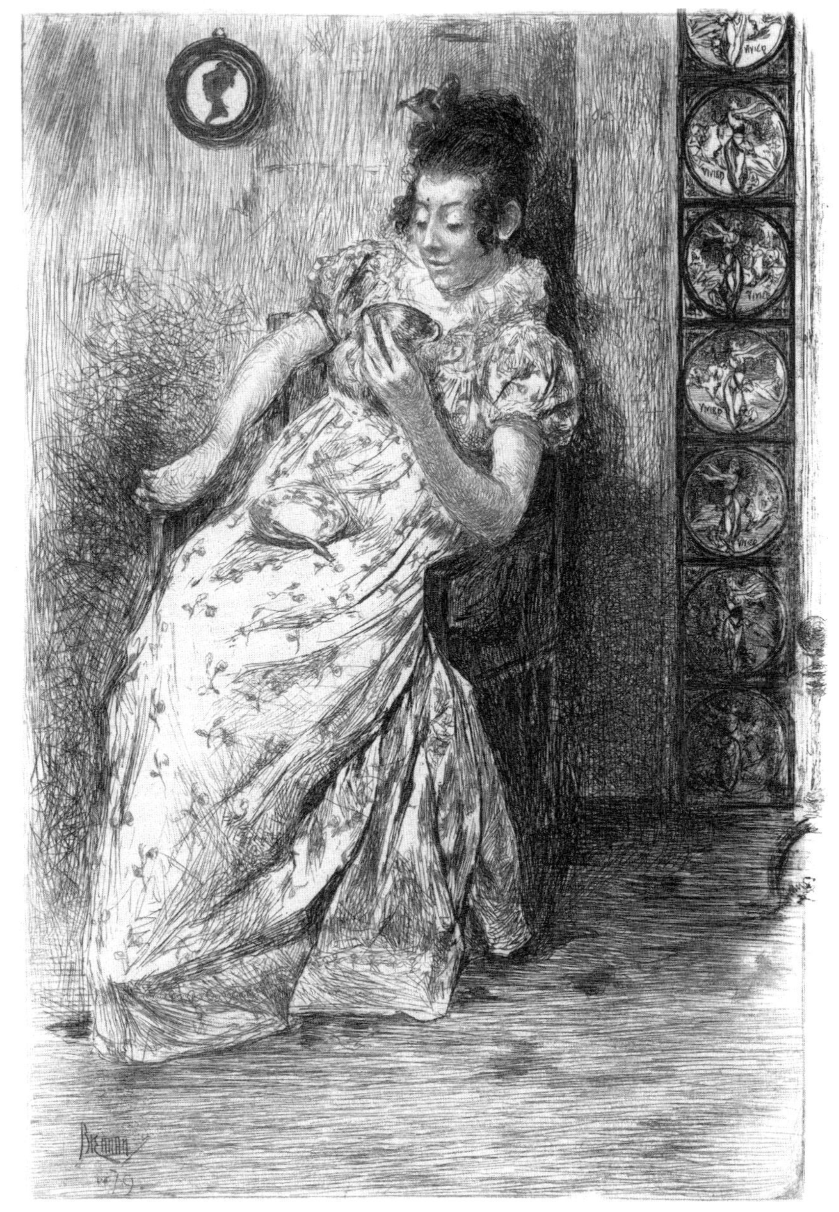

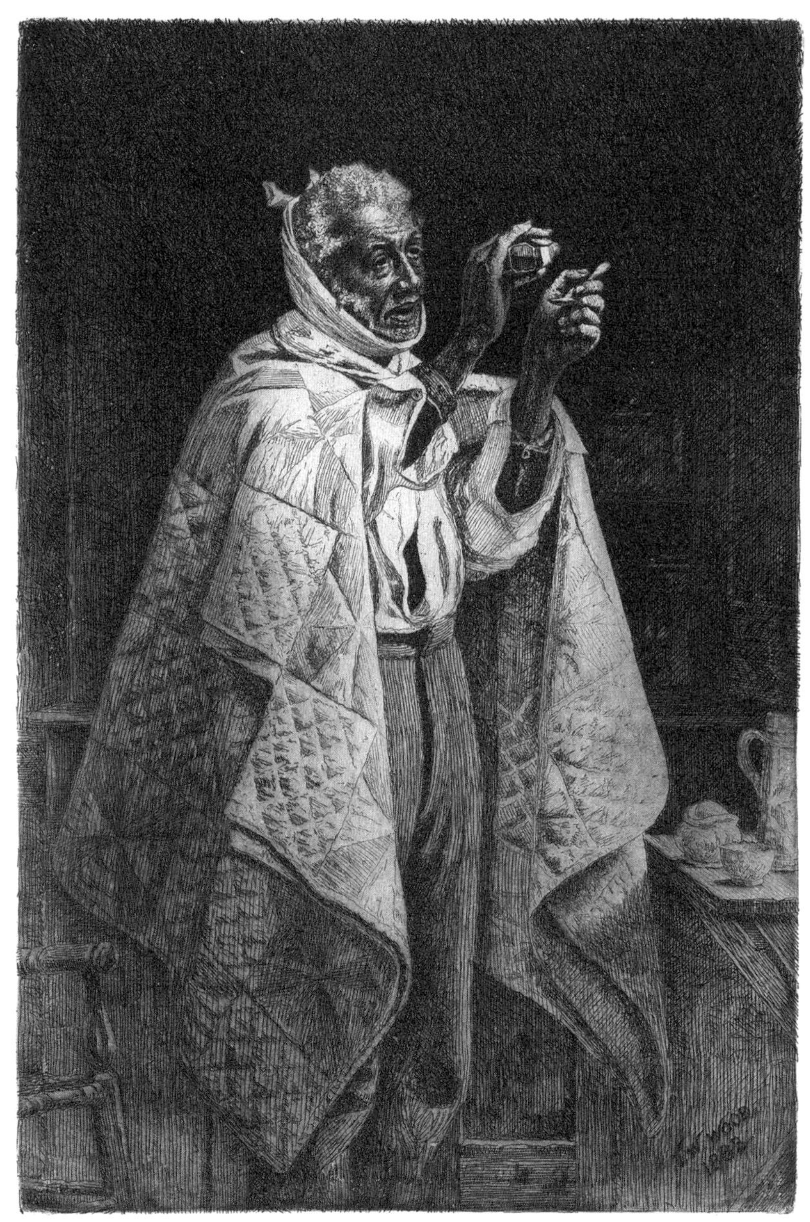

T W WOOD

THOMAS WATERMAN WOOD (1823-1903), a Vermont native, was one of America's greatest genre painters, portraying African Americans as human beings worthy of the American artist as a subject. He lived in Louisville, Kentucky, during the latter years of the Civil War painting portraits and a celebrated set of three works known as *War Episode* or *A Bit of War History.* The triptych depicts a proud black man who enlists in the Union Army and returns home wounded.

There is another possible Kentucky connection: He is said to have studied portraiture in Boston, Massachusetts, with Chester Harding, who was in Kentucky in the 1820s. Wood also studied in Paris, France.

Wood established himself in New York City in 1867, where he was successful with his paintings of American "types," as he phrased it, and prints. He served as president of the National Academy of Design and the American Watercolor Society, and was a founder of the New York Etching Club. He established the T.W. Wood Gallery in his hometown of Montpelier, Vermont; it contains the largest collection of his work.

Accompanying *His Own Doctor* in S.R. Koehler's *Original Etchings by American Artists* (Cassell and Company) is a discussion of "the negro element" in American art. "Nowhere is a richer treasury of subject to be found than in the history and the life of the negro of the United States. Pathos rising to the height of tragedy, humor, the idyll, lie here side by side, waiting only for the hand that is capable of shaping them artistically." Those who did, in the essayist's view, were Eastman Johnson, Winslow Homer, Thomas Hovenden and, of course, Wood. Wood's etching is a reproductive of his painting which enjoyed some success in a National Academy of Design exhibition.

His Own Doctor
etching
1883
11 1/2 x 7 3/4 inches

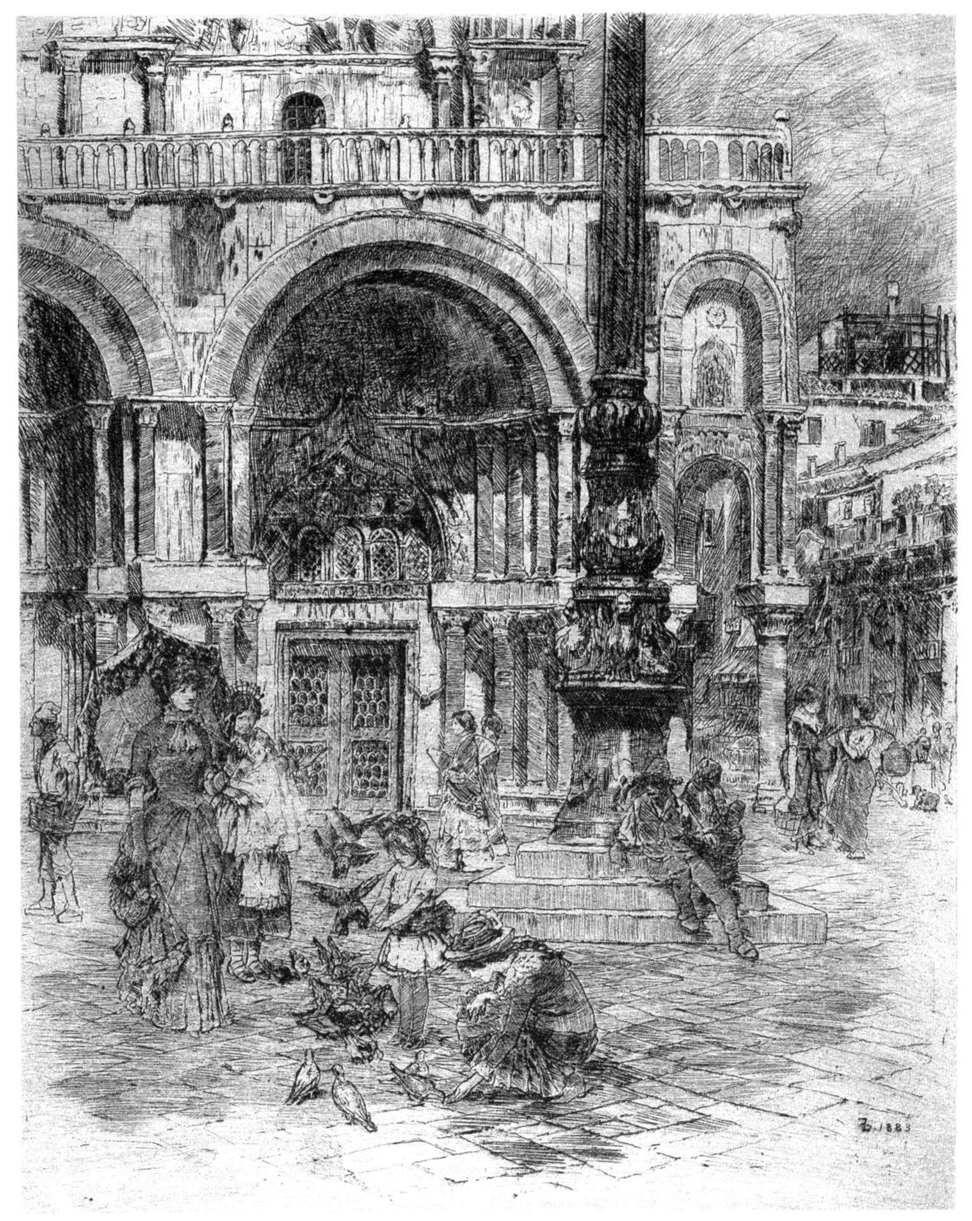

FRANK DUVENECK (1848-1919) was an American painter, printmaker and teacher. He was born in Covington, Kentucky, across the Ohio River from Cincinnati, Ohio, and worked as a church decorator.

In 1870 he traveled to Munich, Germany, to study, a trip he would repeat over two decades. He started a painting class in Europe with a group of students referred to as the "Duveneck Boys." In 1880 in Venice, Italy, Duveneck executed his first etchings and worked with American painter-etcher James Abbott McNeill Whistler, who by then had been etching for over 20 years. Duveneck had successful exhibitions in the United States and Europe throughout this period, including an 1881 etching show in London, Great Britain. He was a member of the Royal Society of Painters-Etchers and Engravers.

Duveneck's teaching career had begun in 1874 at the Ohio Mechanics Institute in Cincinnati, and in 1900 he joined the faculty of the Cincinnati Art Academy, where he became one of the most influential teachers in Cincinnati art history.

As an etcher, "no one has approached him in beauty and meaning of line," Joseph Pennell, American printmaker and Whistler biographer, wrote in his 1919 book *Etchers and Etchings* (Macmillan). "Duveneck for years did little and showed less – fell out of sight in this country – lived his own life, in his own city, in his own way, beloved and respected by all who knew him – and then just before his death found himself a great man."

An *Exhibition of the Work of Frank Duveneck* was held in 1936 by the Cincinnati Art Museum and 30 etchings and several monotypes were displayed.

Piazza di San Marco
etching
1883
13 X 10 1/2 inches

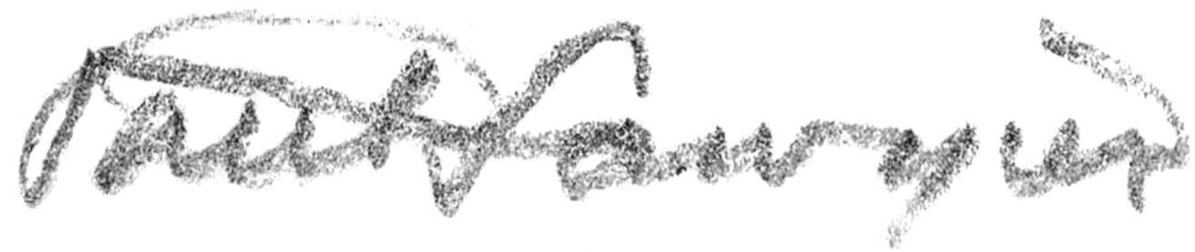

PAUL SAWYIER (1865-1917) is considered by many *the* Kentucky painter. His family moved from Ohio to Frankfort, Kentucky, when he was five years old, and scenes of that city and its environs dominate his art, primarily executed in watercolor. He was one of the few proponents of Impressionism in the Commonwealth at the turn of the century.

His studies in Cincinnati, Ohio, with fellow Kentuckians Thomas Satterwhite Noble and Frank Duveneck and in New York City with Hoosier William Merritt Chase came during the period of the American Etching Revival, the 1880s and 1890s.

In 1887-1888, sources generally agree, Sawyier began engraving on copper and produced several quality prints, all Frankfort scenes. There is no documentation as to why he took up the needle or who might have offered guidance. Two of his best-selling etchings showed Frankfort's old wooden bridge, a covered bridge, which was replaced by an iron structure in 1893. Nostalgia for the old bridge may have explained their popularity, one local newspaper reporting in 1894 that they were being snapped up as Christmas presents.

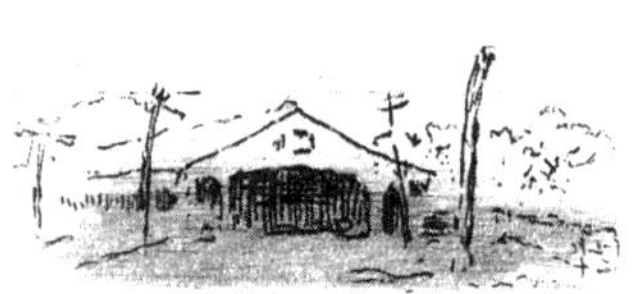

Sawyier used the Frankfort druggist concern of LeCompte and Gayle, to which he was sometimes in debt, to produce his prints. The firm had a Chicago, Illinois, engraving company print the etchings in runs of 50, sold them, had another run done and so on until 1945, when fire destroyed the plates.

As far as is known, Sawyier never produced another print. He moved to New York City in 1913 and continued developing his considerable skill as a painter in oils.

In his 2018 book *Elkhorn: Evolution of a Kentucky Landscape*, Kentucky poet Richard Taylor pronounced Sawyier "our most committed topophiliac, a lover of place whose devotion transcended infatuation and entered a state of profound spiritual attachment."

title unknown
(referred to as *South End Stroll*)
etching
7 1/2 x 12 inches (with remarque)

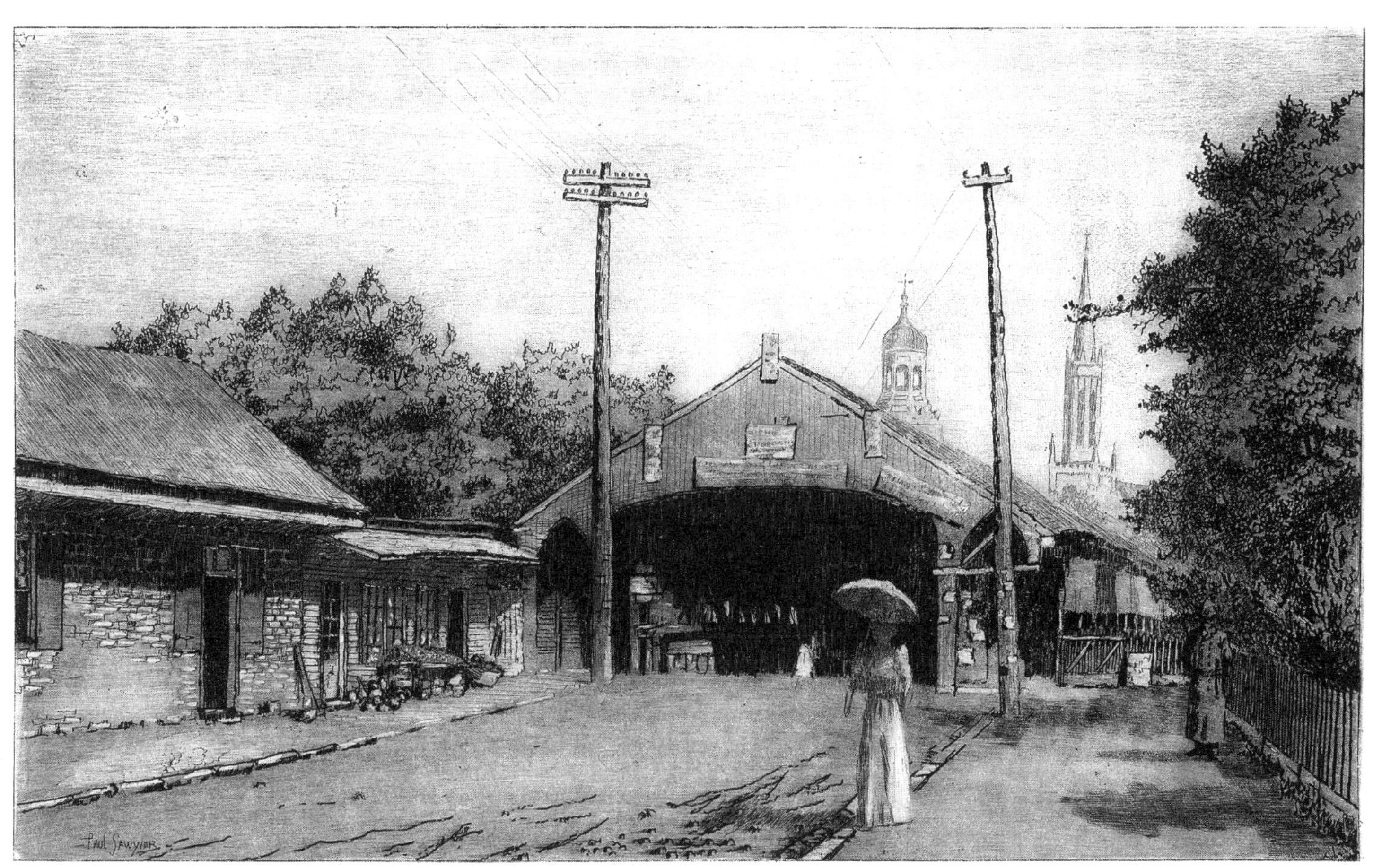
Paul Sawyier

At the turn of the 20th century **LOUISE HOWLAND KING COX** (1865-1945) produced a series of etchings showing famous American sites and genre scenes for the M.F. Tobin Co. of New York City. She signed herself L.H. King. *The Birthplace of Abraham Lincoln* was one of that nostalgic series.

Cox, a native of San Francisco, California, was a teenager living in New York City when she began studying at the National Academy of Design and later at the Art Students League. One of her teachers at the Art Students League was painter Kenyon Cox. A relationship developed, and the two married in 1892. They lived in the city but had a summer home in Cornish, New Hampshire, where they were part of that fabled artist colony. Her husband died in 1919. She lived in Italy and Hawaii, eventually residing in Mount Kisco, New York.

Cox was a known as a painter of children, a muralist, a designer of stained glass, an illustrator and a printmaker. Among her prizes were a bronze medal at the 1900 Paris Exposition and a silver medal at the 1901 Pan-American Exposition in Buffalo, New York

Among her other large etchings of the Lincoln's *Birthplace* period were *The Little Church Around the Corner, Down on the Suwannee River* and *The Birthplace of Howard Payne,* all dated 1897 and all published by the M.F. Tobin art-publishing company of New York City. The Lincoln etching was being offered as a premium for subscribers to *The Home Magazine* in 1907.

The Birthplace of Abraham Lincoln
etching
1897
13 x 17 3/4 inches

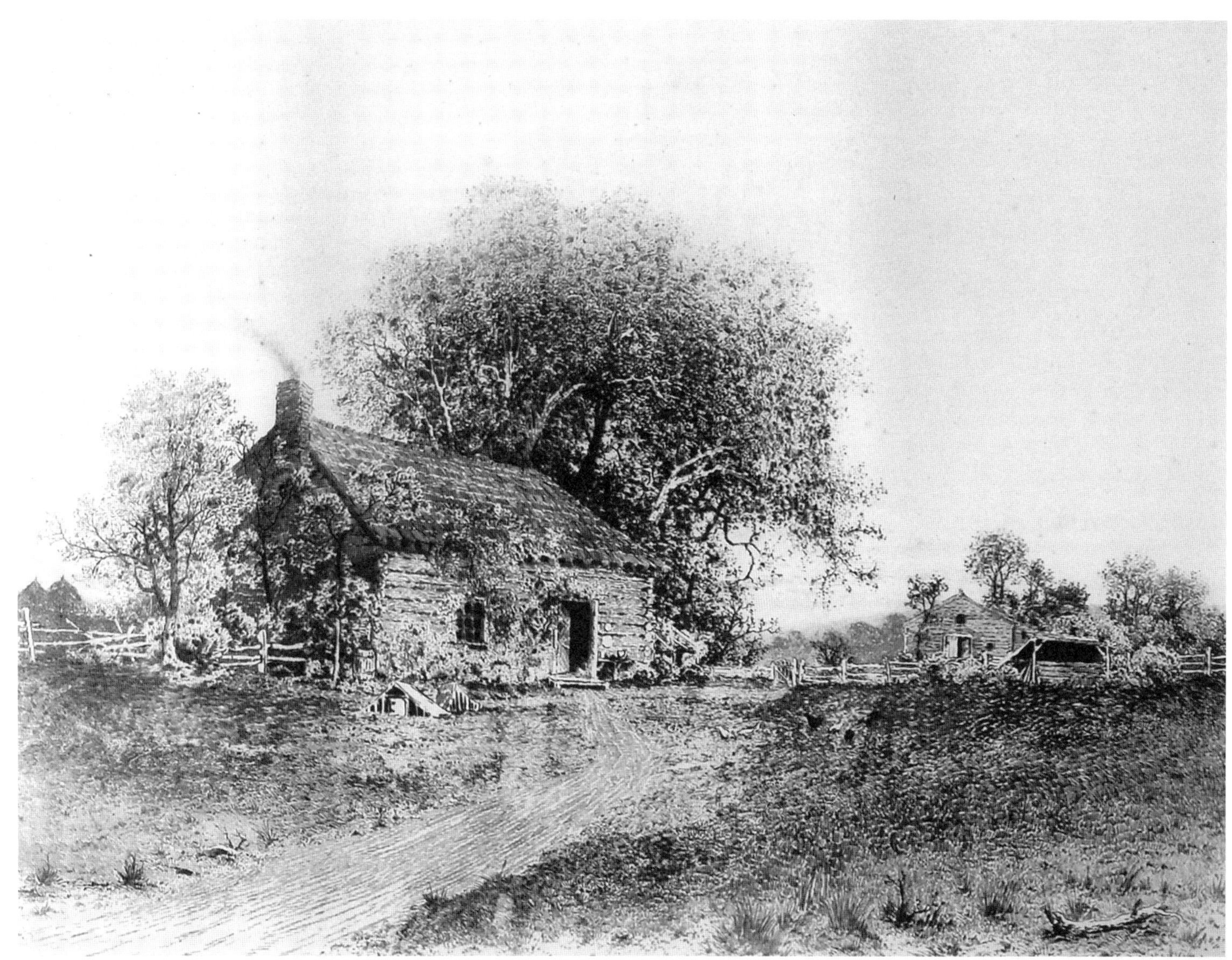

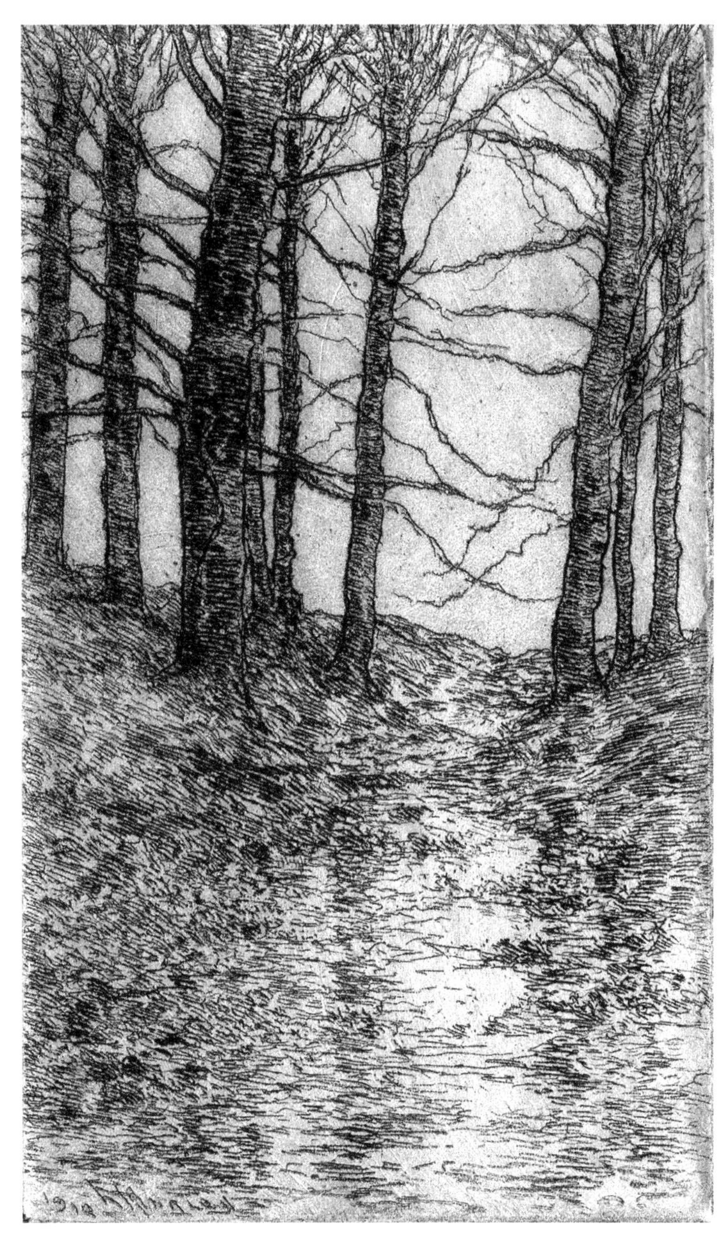

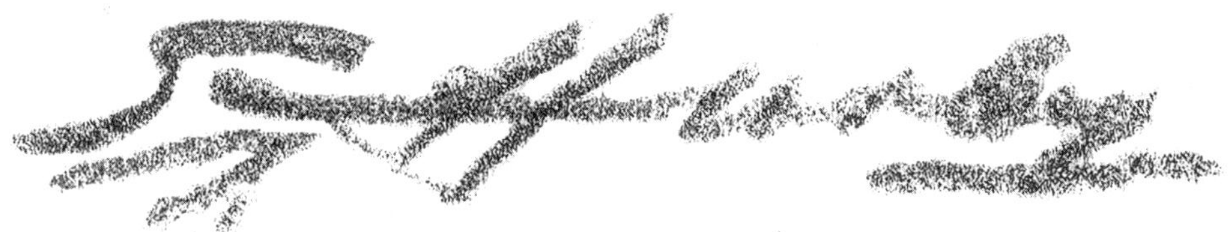

EDWARD TIMOTHY HURLEY was a Cincinnati, Ohio, artist and pottery decorator.

Hurley (1869-1950) was born in Cincinnati, graduated from St. Xavier College (Xavier University) and trained with painter-etcher Frank Duveneck at the Cincinnati Art Academy. He worked at the Rookwood Pottery Co. for 52 years, starting in 1896. He also created and sold art supplies under his name.

As a painter and printmaker, he captured life in Cincinnati and on both sides of the Ohio River in the 1920s and 1930s, definitely placing himself in the American Scene movement. He lived for a time in Northern Kentucky and traveled through the state sketching such scenes as Cumberland Falls and Federal Hill (My Old Kentucky Home) for etchings.

His memberships included local arts clubs such as the Crafters' Club and the Duveneck Society of Painters and Sculptors. His work is in institutional collections in Pittsburgh, Pennsylvania, Brooklyn, New York, Washington, D.C., Detroit, Michigan, and more. He took a gold medal at the Louisiana Purchase Exposition in St. Louis, Missouri, in 1904.

title unknown
etching
1912
4 1/2 x 2 3/4 inches

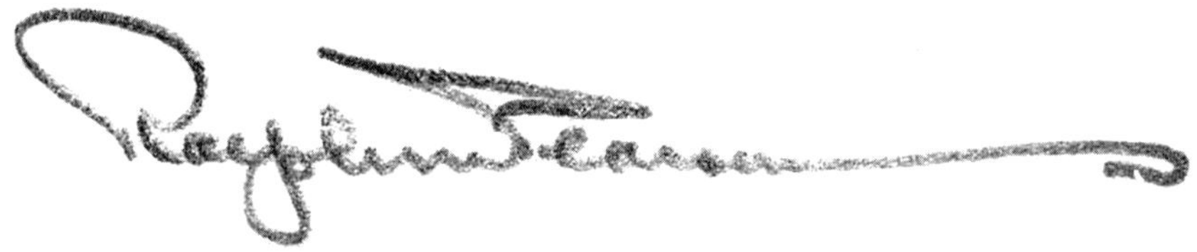

RALPH MOSHER PEARSON's *Lincoln's Birthplace* was part of an etching series dedicated to Abraham Lincoln. Other plates in *Lincoln* included a view of the Lincoln family home in Springfield, Illinois, and a depiction of a Lincoln statue, *Lincoln Monument*. *Lincoln's Birthplace* is in the collection of the Fine Arts Museums of San Francisco (California).

Lincoln's Birthplace
drypoint
1915
11 3/8 x 9 1/4 inches

Pearson (1883-1958) was an Iowa native who moved to the big city, Chicago, Illinois, started a profitable business and pursued his artistic interests at the School of the Art Institute of Chicago. He was influenced by a frequent visitor to Chicago, celebrated American etcher Joseph Pennell. Pearson quickly became involved in the founding of the Chicago Society of Etchers. His etchings sold, and he would publish two more series, *Toilers of the City* and *Chicago Landmarks*.

In 1913 Pearson came face to face with Modernism in the *Armory Show* at its Chicago stop. He headed for New York City and attended the Modern Art School. The artist colony at Taos, New Mexico, beckoned, then California. By the late 1920s he was back in New York, where he had teaching and writing careers. In 1952 he published *The New Art Education,* considered to this day a classic in art education.

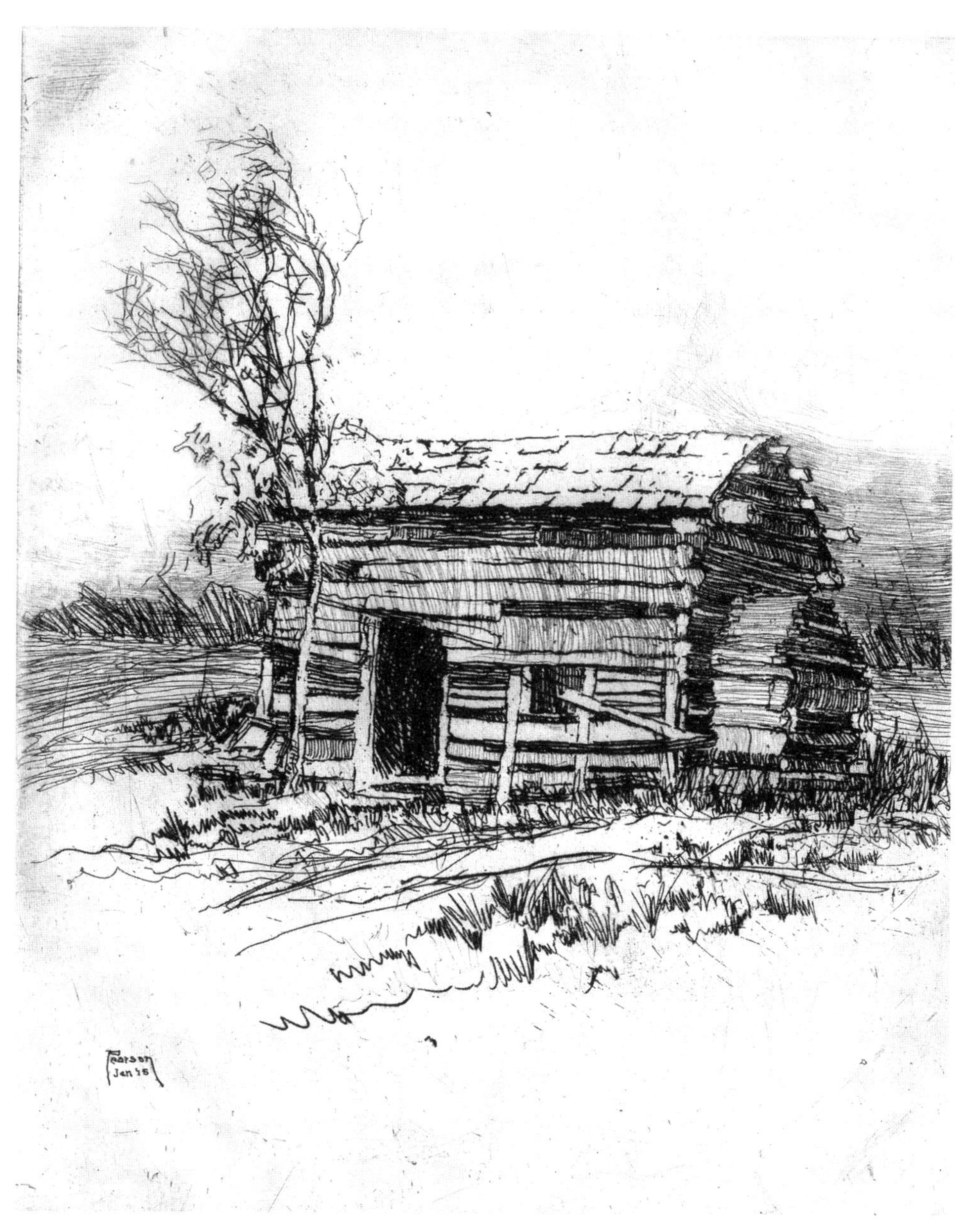
Pearson

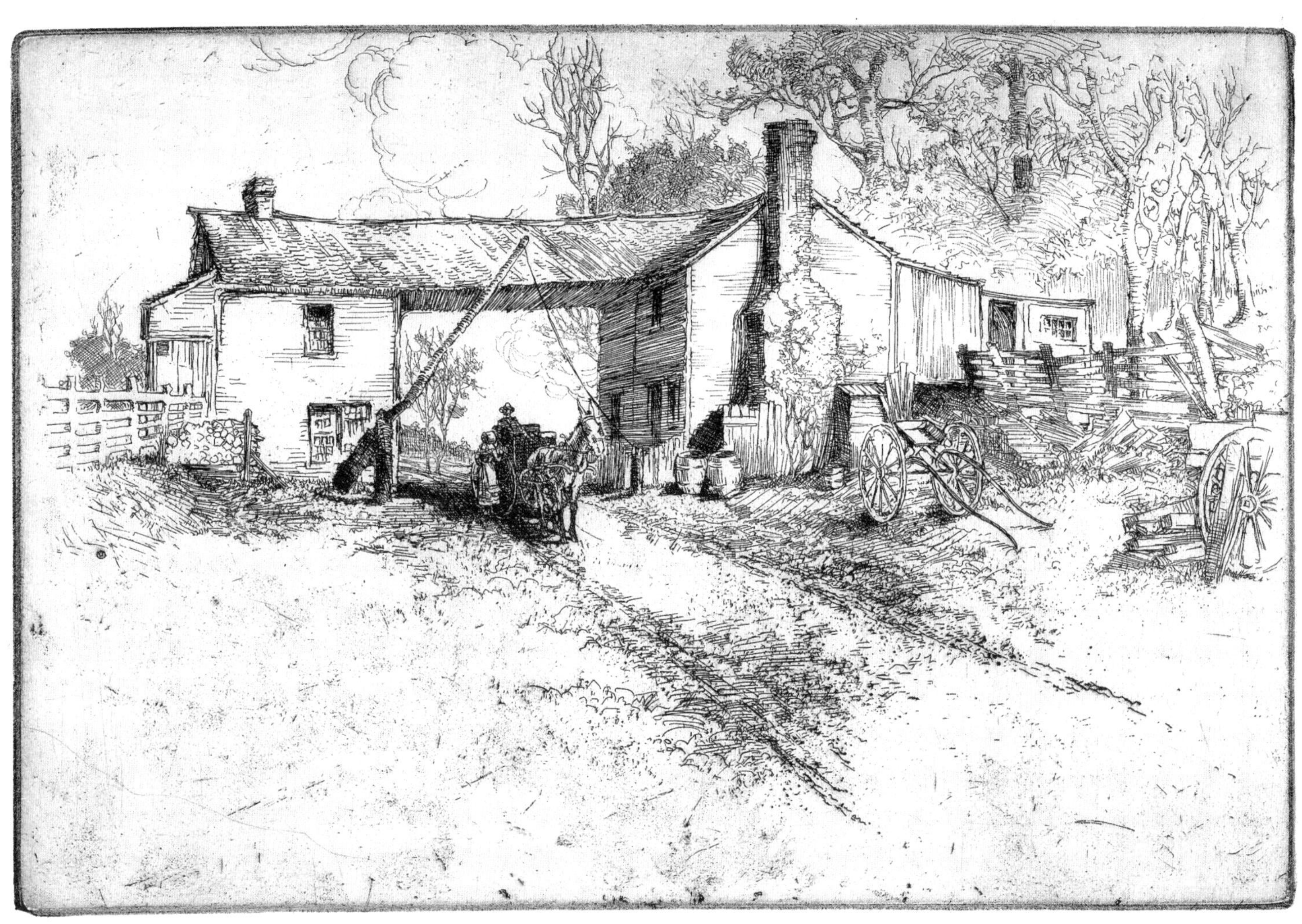

In 1919 **ALEXANDER JOSEF VAN LESHOUT** installed an etching press at his Louisville School of Art, and the area saw a flowering of printmaking that continued into the 1940s.

Van Leshout (1868-1930) was a native of Illinois. He studied at the School of the Art Institute of Chicago and at the Art Students League in New York City. He spent time in Paris, France, and in the Netherlands, where his father was born.

He came to Louisville in 1914 as a cartoonist for the *Courier-Journal* and the *Louisville Times*. He came with some experience, having worked for newspapers in Chicago, Milwaukee, Wisconsin, Philadelphia, Pennsylvania, Washington, D.C., New York and Los Angeles, California. He spent about seven years at the *Courier-Journal* and the *Times*, then went to work for the *Louisville Herald-Post* part-time. He founded the Louisville School of Art in 1919, serving as its president and director. Well-known Louisville artists were involved in the school. Van Leshout also taught at the first Louisville art school for black children, established in the West End by educator Caroline B. Bourgard in the late 1920s.

Van Leshout showed 16 prints at the Louisville Artists League's 1919 exhibition at the Louisville Free Public Library. He exhibited in Louisville and in Chicago at the Art Institute through the 1920s. He took awards at All-Southern Art and Southern States Art League exhibitions. One of his etchings is in the Smithsonian American Art Museum, a gift of the Chicago Society of Etchers. His *Kentucky Toll Gate,* opposite, was shown in the 1925 Louisville Art Association's *Exhibition of the Work of Louisville Artists* at the library.

Van Leshout's oeuvre also includes scenes of the American West. While working in Milwaukee, he traveled to South Dakota and recorded the hard lives of the homesteaders and the Indians. In Edna Kohl's 1938 book *Land of the Burnt Thigh*, Van Leshout is said to have "made a success of his Indian art" because he had come "to know these people (the Sioux) better than any of us."

Kentucky Toll Gate
etching
8 3/4 x 13 1/8 inches

Edward Fisk

Modernist **EDWARD FRANKLIN FISK** brought that cosmopolitan art movement to Lexington, Kentucky, in 1926 when he began teaching at the University of Kentucky.

Fisk (1886-1944) was a native of New York City and received his early training there. He studied at the Art Students League, National Academy of Design and Ashcan School painter Robert Henri's independent studio. He was familiar with the art scene in Greenwich Village and Provincetown, Massachusetts. His friends included playwright Eugene O'Neill.

Exposure to the Fauvists followed in Paris, France, where Fisk palled around with fellow Modernists Stuart Davis, Charles Demuth and Marsden Hartley and attended American author and art patron Gertrude Stein's legendary salon. Fisk was represented by several Manhattan galleries.

He became interested in printmaking in his late 40s, according to Rachel Sadinsky in *Edward Fisk American Modernist* (University of Kentucky). He "mastered the difficult processes of etching and mezzotint, producing prints which are impressive for their range of tone and intimate subject matter," she opined. Further study in printmaking came with a trip to Great Britain. Back in Lexington, Fisk was awarded a grant to promote the graphic arts on campus and off. He accumulated books, prints and slides, which were available to women's and civic clubs, and toured the state with programs on the subject.

Fisk's first one-man show in Kentucky came in 1935 at the university and the Speed Art Museum in Louisville. He still exhibited in New York, where he was involved in choosing art for the 1939 World's Fair. An exhibition in England in 1940 was his last lifetime show. The University of Kentucky mounted a retrospective, with catalog, in 1998.

title unknown
block print
1928
5 1/4 x 7 1/2 inches

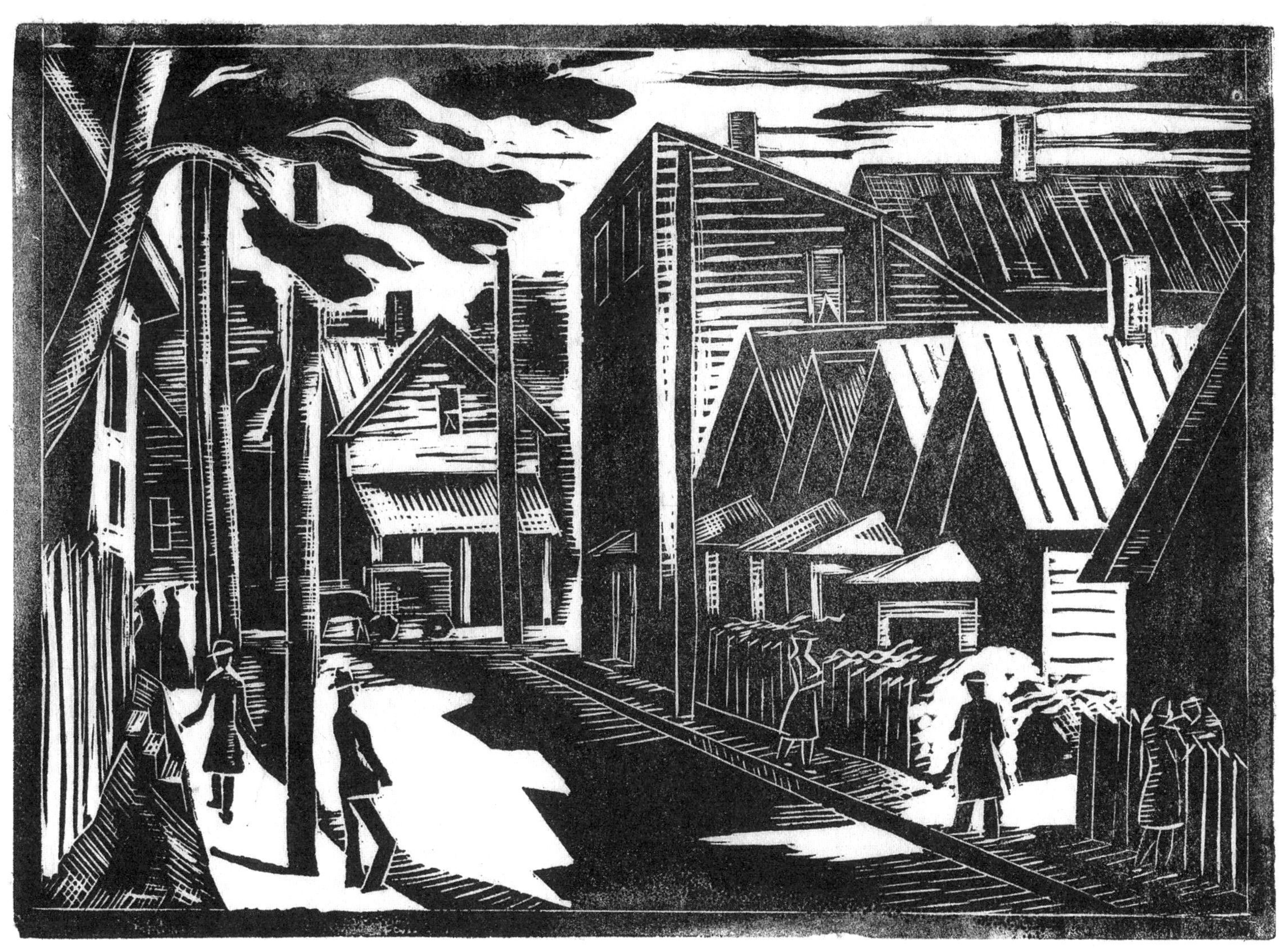

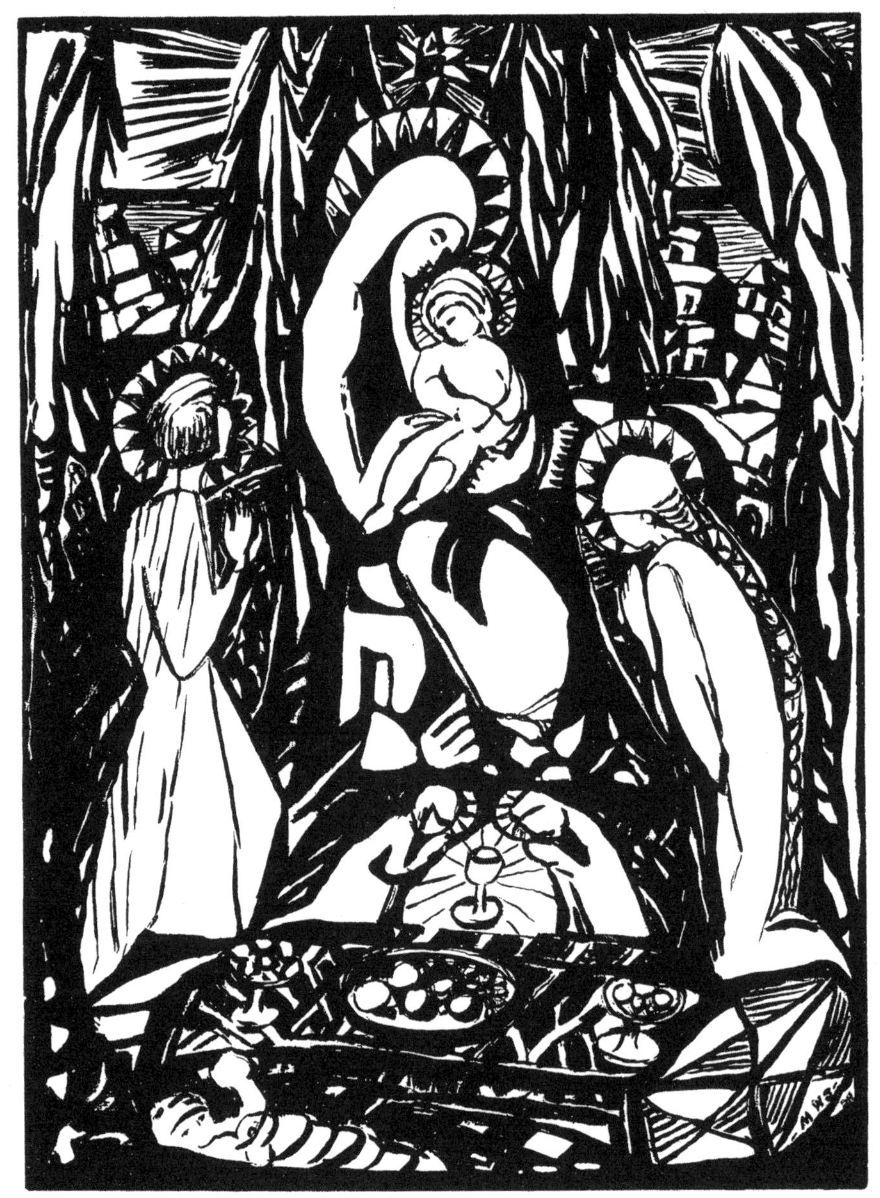

Mary W Schachner

Information about Louisvillian **MARY WELLER SCHACHNER**'s artistic endeavors is hard to come by.

Schachner (1869-1956) was associated with the Louisville Handicraft Guild and the Louisville Art Center, serving on the center's board in 1939 when the organization opened its new facility on South First Street.

She was a doctor's wife. Her husband, Dr. August Schachner, founded a medical library for black physicians in Louisville and was widely credited with helping preserve the history of pioneer Danville, Kentucky, doctor Ephraim McDowell.

Mrs. Schachner exhibited in the Louisville Art Association's 1925 *Exhibition of the Work of Louisville Artists* at the Louisville Free Public Library, and in 1930 she showed a print and two other pieces in the art association's *Fourth Annual Exhibition of Kentucky and Southern Indiana Arts* at the Speed Art Museum.

She and her daughter, Katherine Schachner, apparently shared a love for art. The daughter showed in a 1930 Provincetown (Massachusetts) Art Association show. Back in Louisville, she appeared in the 1931 *No-Jury Exhibition for Members Only of the Louisville Art Association* and the next year appeared in the art association's *Fifth Annual Exhibition of Kentucky and Southern Indiana Arts,* both at the Speed. Katherine went on to become a well-known artist in New York City.

Mother and daughter are listed on the *Kentucky Women Artists* website and the Johnson Collection's *Directory of Southern Women Artists*.

title unknown
block print
1929
12 x 9 inches

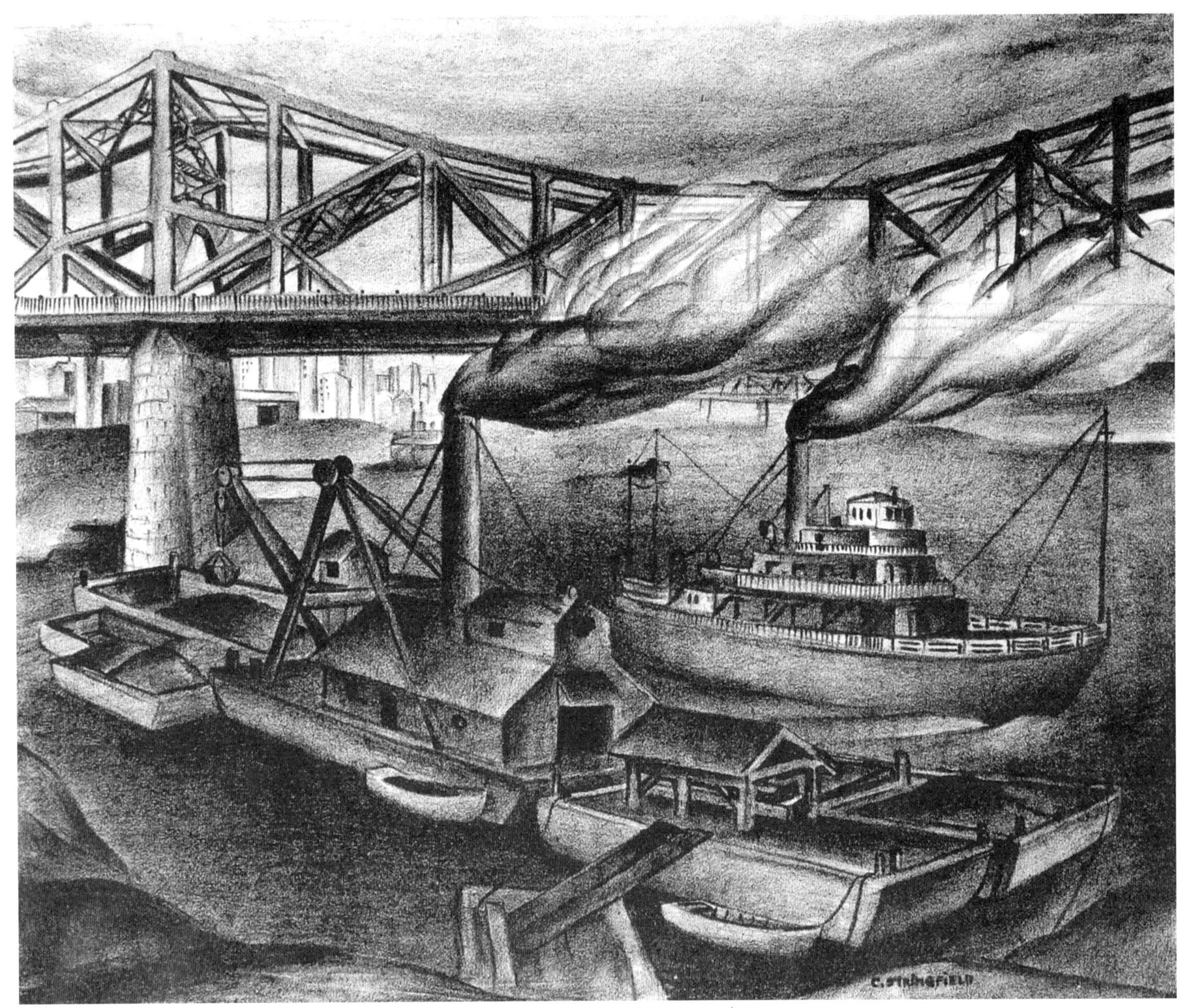
C. STRINGFIELD

Clyde Stringfield

CLYDE H. STRINGFIELD (1907-1981) was born in Ballard County, Kentucky, the son of a miner, and came to Louisville to train in commercial art. He attended the Ahrens Trade School, A.J. Van Leshout's Louisville School of Art and the Louisville Art Center. Additional training came at the School of Illustration in New York City.

A *Courier-Journal* article in 1949 talked of Stringfield's "vast experience as a commercial artist" and cited his years as the assistant art director of the *Louisville Herald-Post* newspaper and as an artist for The Courier-Journal and Louisville Times Co. He appears to have been most active as a commercial and fine artist in the 1930s.

He illustrated a *Courier-Journal* series of historic Kentucky homes called *Domestic Pageant in Old Kentucky* in 1935. One of the features, on the Wolf Pen Mill in Jefferson County, was illustrated with a lithograph. That same year 25 pen-and-inks and lithographs of those structures were shown at the Woman's Club of Louisville. He also did a series of pen-and-ink sketches of the historic buildings in Harrodsburg, Kentucky, for *The Louisville Times* in connection with the dedication of the Pioneer Memorial there by President Franklin D. Roosevelt in 1934.

As a fine artist, he had watercolors, drawings and lithographs in such shows as the Louisville Art Association's *Kentucky and Southern Indiana Artists Exhibition* at the Speed Art Museum in 1931 and 1933 and the *No-Jury Exhibition by Members Only of The Louisville Art Association* at the Speed, also in 1931. He had an exhibition in 1934 in the Fine Arts Gallery at the University of Illinois (Urbana-Champaign), and in 1936 another in Harrodsburg in connection with the Kentucky Federation of Women's Clubs.

Stringfield moved to New York City to specialize in magazine-cover work. He was a member of the Advertising Club of New York and the Kit Kat Club. He returned to Ballard County in 1943 to farm and freelance, living in Barlow. His depiction of a duck hunter was the December 1948 cover of *Outdoorsman Magazine.* He continued painting and exhibiting, taking a prize at a Woman's Club of Paducah show in 1962.

New Bridge
lithograph
circa 1929
12 3/4 x 15 1/2 inches

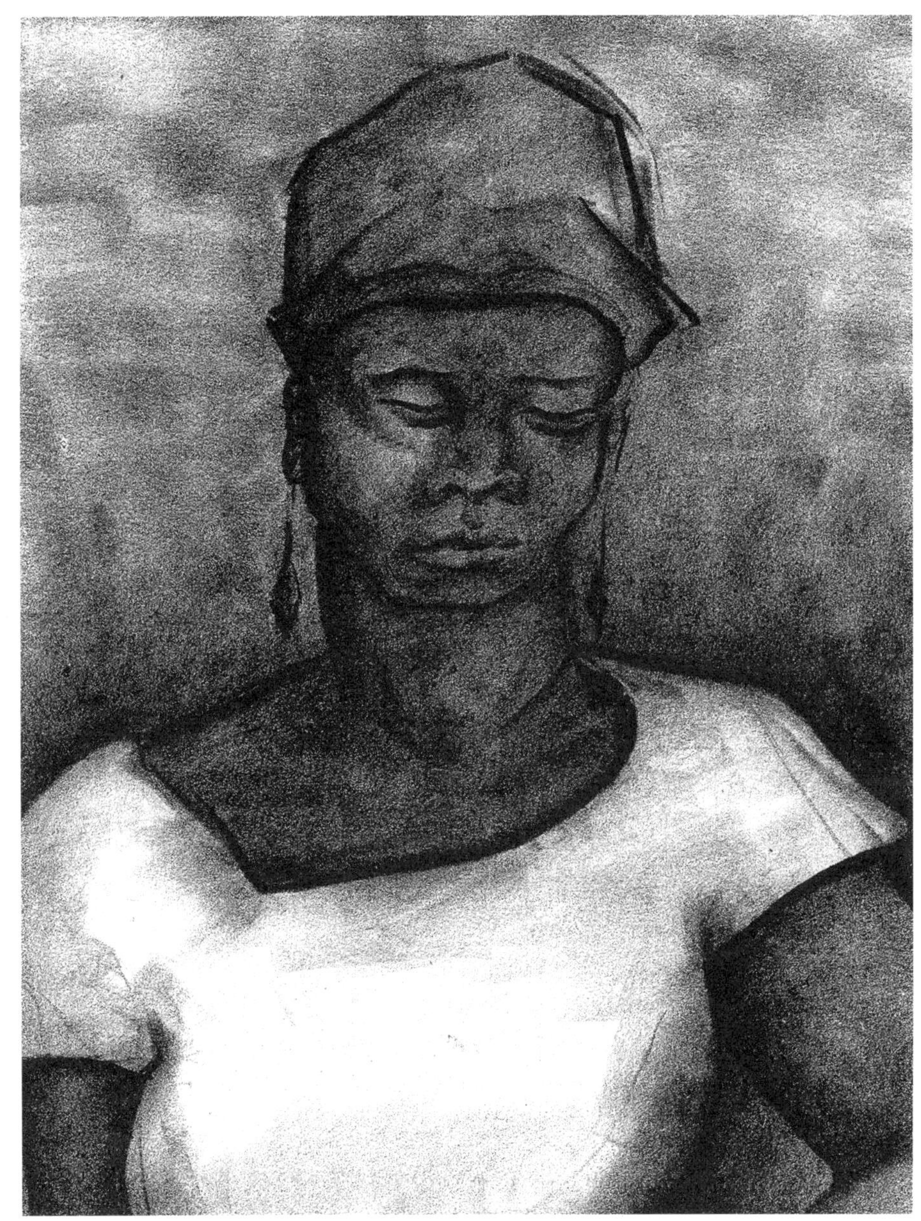

ARTHUR D. ALLEN (1879-1949) came from a prominent Louisville family. He and his wife, fellow artist Jane Mengel Allen (1888-1952), were both connected with the Belknap Hardware and Mengel companies. The library of their estate outside Louisville in Glenview was considered the most beautiful room in the city at that time. The couple were philanthropists and major supporters of the arts.

Arthur Allen took up art at the age of 45, in 1924. A visit to the Provincetown, Massachusetts, art colony inspired him, and instruction from American Regionalist James R. Hopkins, an Ohio native, grounded him. He reportedly left the business world entirely to devote himself to art. Success followed with shows at the Frank K.M. Rehm Gallery in New York City, which also exhibited the early work of American Modernist Edward Hopper. Allen's work combines American Regionalist and modernist traits and reflects his travels, with scenes from Cape Cod, Massachusetts, Venice, Italy, the Caribbean, Mexico and the Southwestern United States.

Critics considered Allen a landscapist, one of a group in Louisville in the first half of the 20th century, including Morris Belknap, Dorothy and Norman Kohlhepp and Lucy Diecks.

illegible title
lithograph
edition 12
1929
12 1/2 x 9 3/4 inches

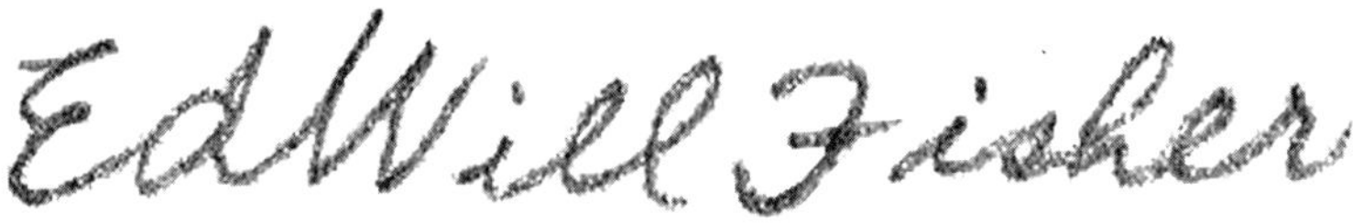

EdWill Fisher

CHARLES EDWILL FISHER (1896-1960) was a Minneapolis, Minnesota, commercial artist who etched as a hobby.

He was born in Rockport, Indiana, but "always claimed Kentucky as his birthplace," according to his daughter, Cheri Skrukud of Nisswa, Minnesota. She added that he "must have spent hours as a young boy sitting and enjoying the Ohio River." That sentiment was echoed in a 1937 profile published in a University of Minnesota publication: "Many of the most delightful of Mr. Fisher's plates have been made from his early-day sketches of the life and people along the Ohio river ... particularly the negro. These subjects are near and dear to his heart."

The family moved to Minneapolis while Fisher was a child. He served in World War I and developed his interest in etching watching French artists documenting the war for the government. He would exhibit his French etchings in 1929.

Fishing on the Ohio River
drypoint
7 1/2 x 9 inches

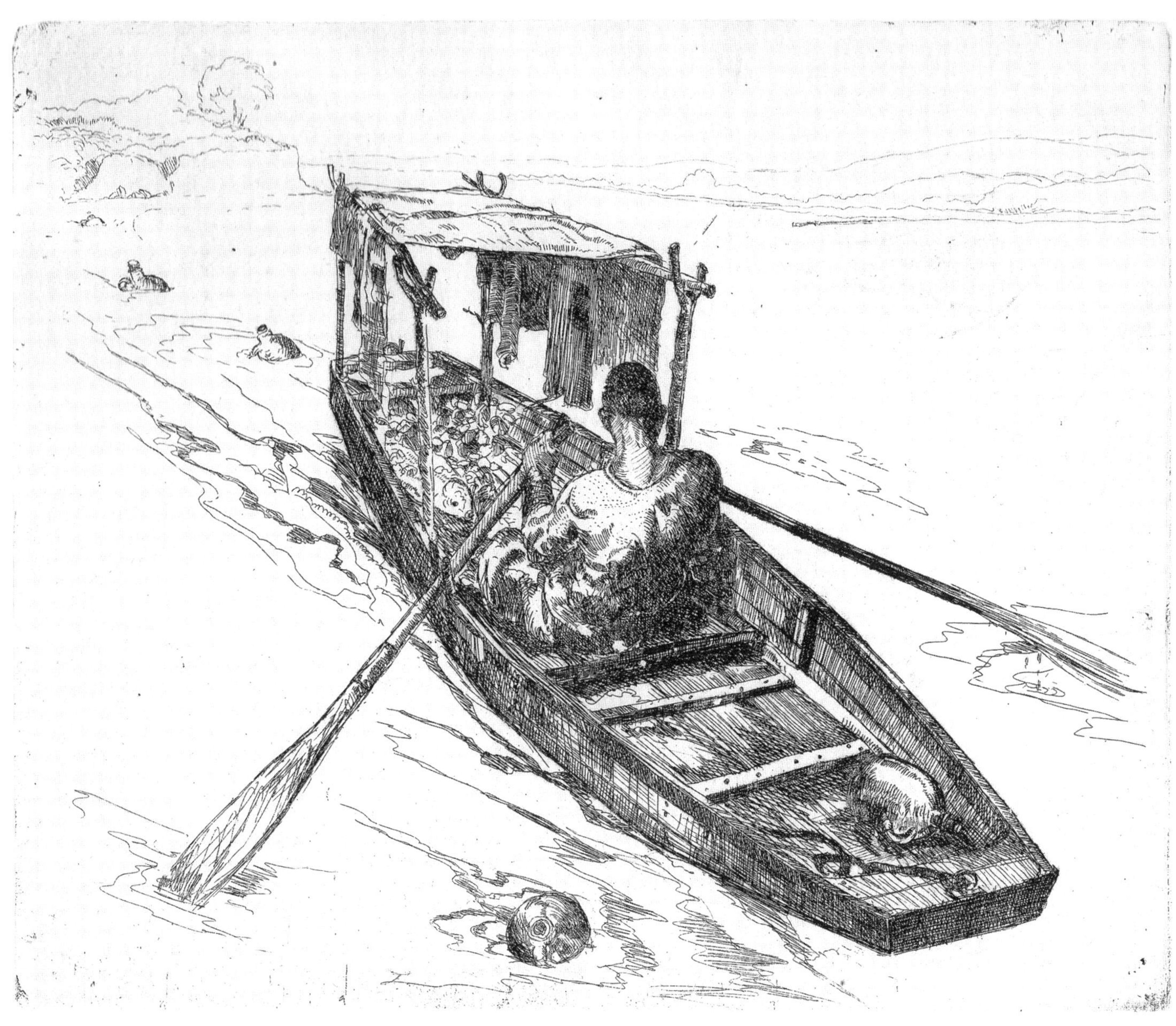

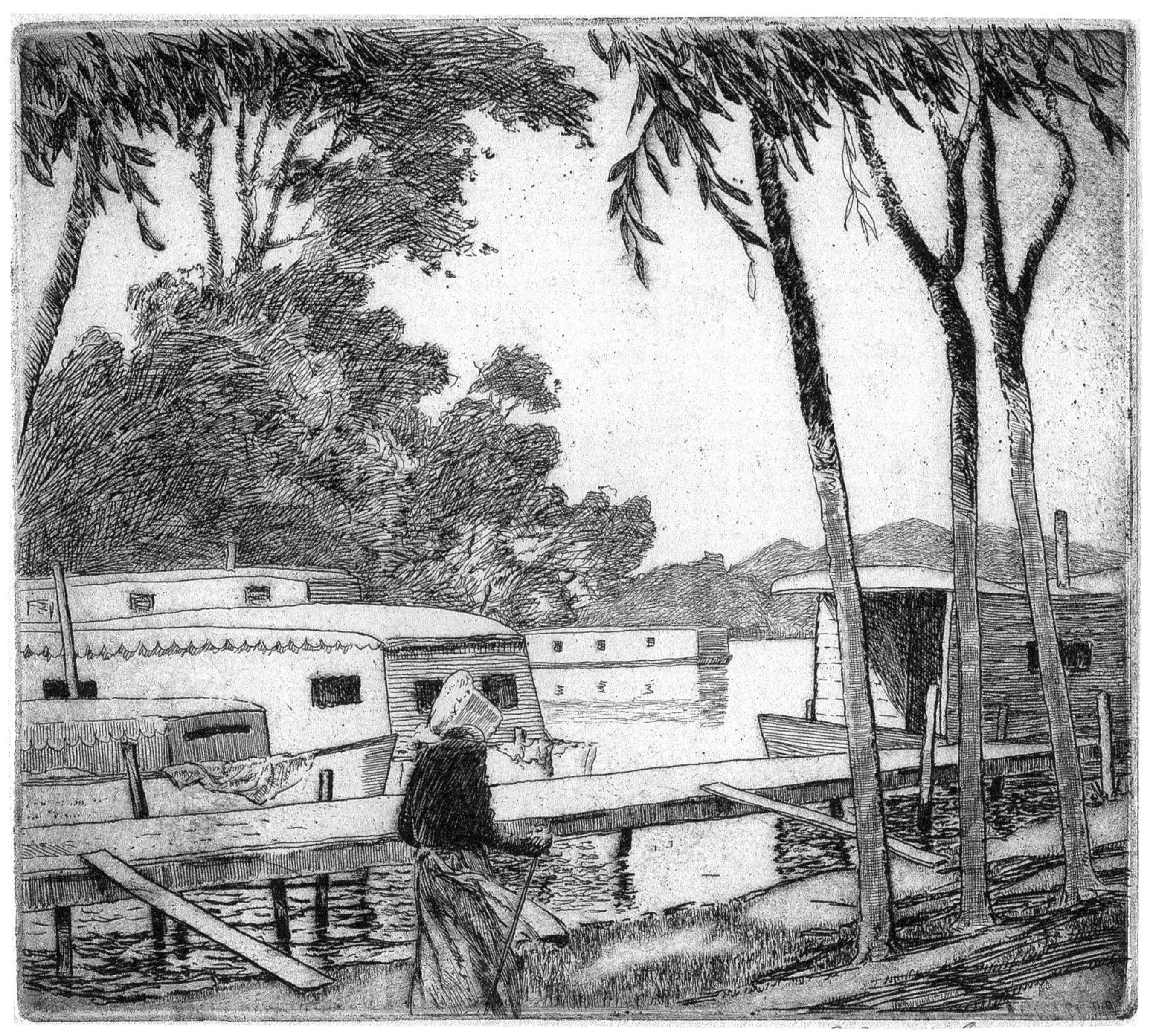

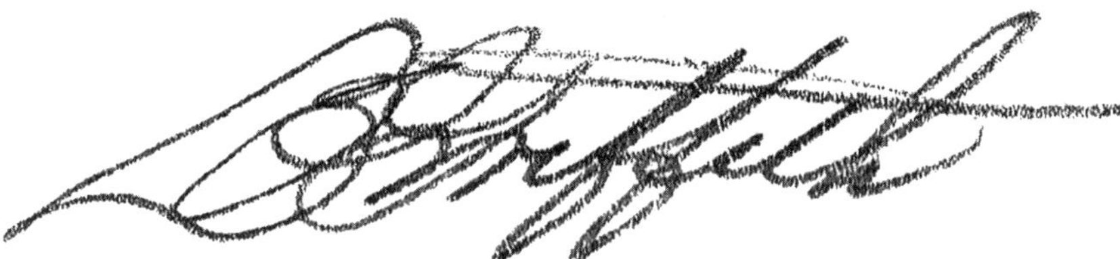

Painter and printmaker **LOUIS OSCAR GRIFFITH** (1875-1956) is known for work in Indiana, Texas and Louisiana.

He was born in Indiana and raised in Texas, where he received his first art instruction with revered landscape painter Frank Reaugh. He studied at the St. Louis (Missouri) School and Museum of Fine Arts (St. Louis Art Museum), then moved to Chicago, Illinois. He studied at the School of the Art Institute of Chicago and found work as an illustrator for an engraving company. A trip to Europe in 1908 increased his painting and printmaking skills.

Griffith became an integral part of the robust Chicago art scene as a member of the Palette and Chisel Club and a charter member of the Chicago Society of Etchers. He exhibited at the Art Institute, and his color aquatints took a bronze medal at the 1915 Panama-Pacific International Exposition in San Francisco, California. In 1916 he visited New Orleans and other locations in the South, including Charleston, South Carolina, producing etchings, color aquatints and paintings.

Palette and Chisel members had discovered Brown County, Indiana, and Griffith's exposure to the picturesque landscape and people resulted in his moving there in 1922 and becoming part of the nascent artist colony. He returned to Texas from time to time and maintained a winter studio in Dallas in the 1920s.

Griffith showed his prints throughout the 1930s and 1940s, for the most part in Indiana. He was an award-winning exhibitor in the Hoosier Salon, and the H. Lieber Co. in Indianapolis regularly showed his work. Lieber had a retrospective in 1943, and the Division of Graphic Arts at the Smithsonian Institution in Washington, D.C., had a show of his prints in 1945.

The Kentucky Side depicts a community of houseboats and shanty-boats on the Kentucky side of the Ohio River. Louisville's shanty-boat phenomenon in the early 20th century attracted established artists from Illinois, Ohio and Indiana.

The Kentucky Side
drypoint
edition number 2
6 x 6 7/8 inches

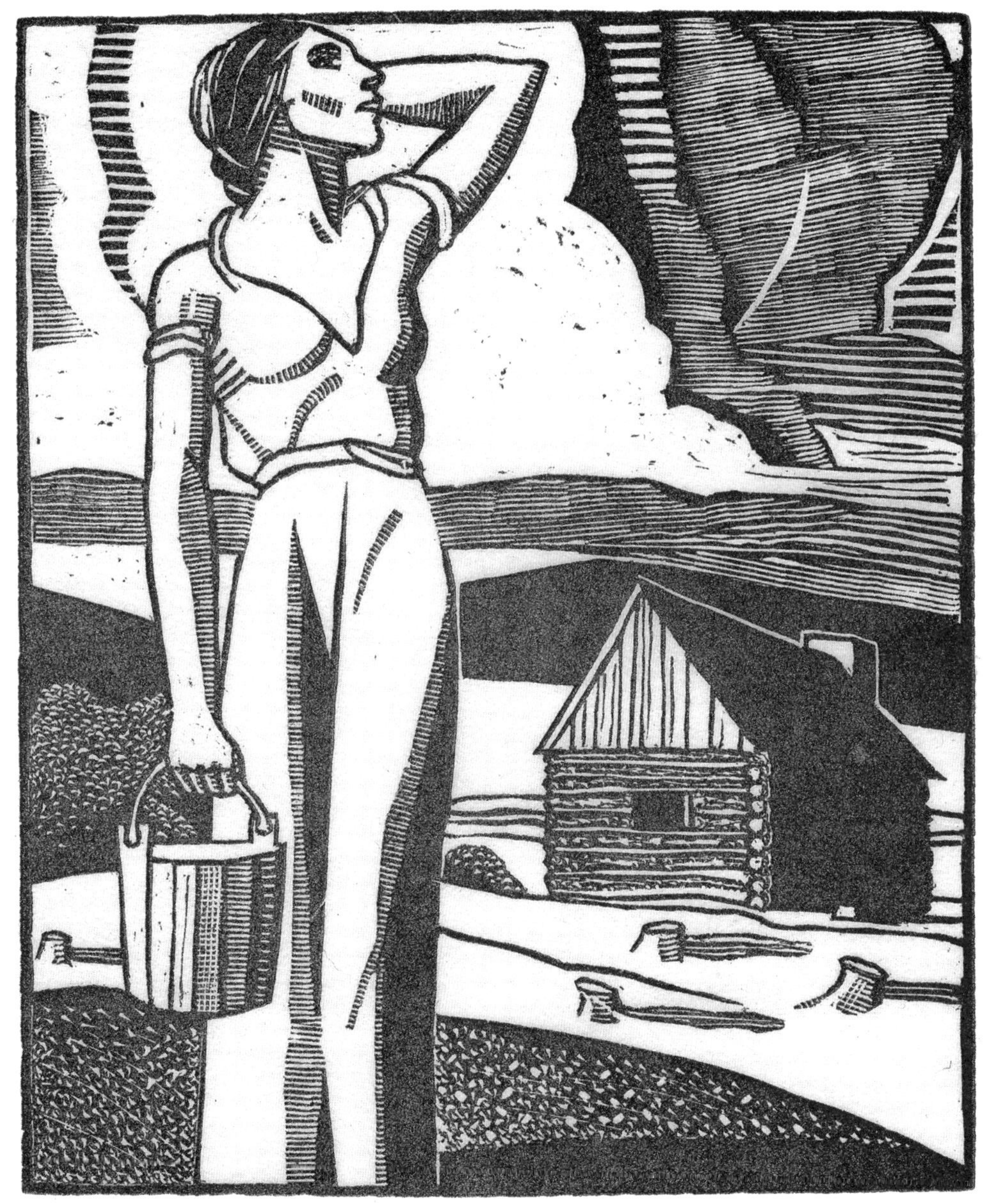

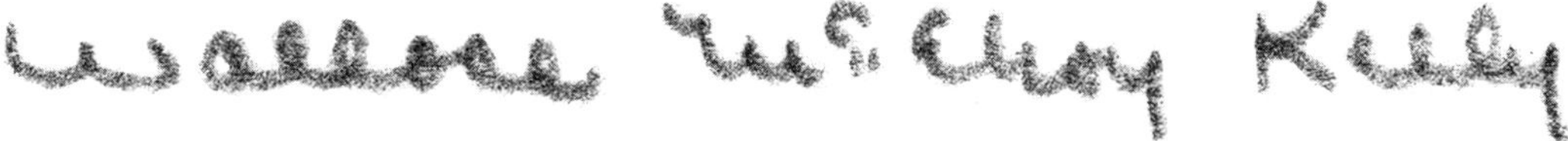

Award-winning novelist and moviemaker **WALLACE MCELROY KELLY** was a prolific artist who, along with Malcolm Arnett of Henderson, Kentucky, created some of the best WPA-era images of life in Kentucky.

Kelly (1910-1988) was a native of Lebanon and lived there most of his life. He attended Centre College in Danville, Kentucky, and the Cincinnati (Ohio) Art Academy. He moved to New York City in 1929 to work as an illustrator. He returned home to help run the family newspaper when his publisher father died. In 1936 he returned to New York to study photography, returned to Lebanon, opened a photo studio and wrote a novel, *Days Are as Grass,* which came out in 1941 and won the Alfred A. Knopf Fellowship in Fiction. Kelly served in World War II in the Pacific Theater as a medic and came back home after the war. He was described as a shy man who worked at home.

Kelly made several films between 1930 and 1950, and his 1938 "home movie" of a day in the life of the Kelly family in Lebanon, *Our Day,* was named to the National Film Registry in 2007.

As a printmaker, Kelly's style varied, from American Regionalist to surreal to abstract. So did his paintings. He sometimes painted on glass, a technique also used by fellow Kentucky painter Harlan Hubbard, who also died in 1988.

In 2009 the Capital Gallery in Frankfort, Kentucky, had an exhibition *Works on Paper / Wallace Kelly / Silkscreens, Lino-cuts, Ink Resist / & Watercolor*. A color linocut of *Pioneer Woman* was in that show.

Pioneer Woman
block print
edition 1/15
6 x 5 inches

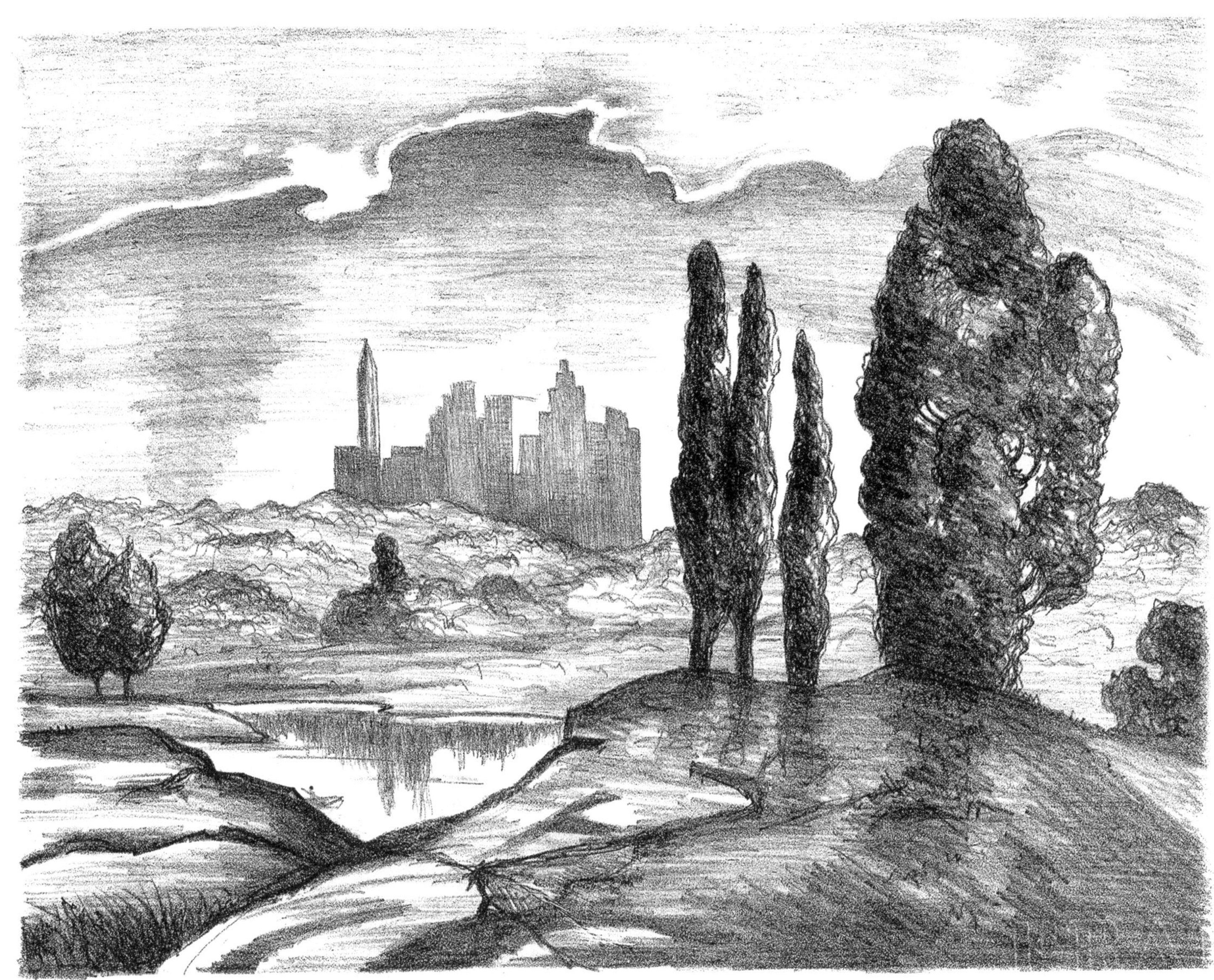

Nellie Schanzenbacher

Louisville native **NELLIE SCHANZENBACHER** (1866-1961) was active in the local art scene for the first four decades of the 20th century.

She honed the talent that developed from childhood by spending three years at the turn of the century in New York City, studying with William Merritt Chase and Robert Henri at the Art Students League. She excelled in the Chase still-life class.

"Miss Nellie" listed herself as a professional artist in the *Louisville City Directory* starting in 1901 and put on her first one-woman show in 1909 in the Courier-Journal Building. She quickly established herself and in 1921 was one of five artists in a *Courier-Journal* photo feature, "Mornings with Women Artists." The other four were Eunice Alden Walker, Gertrude Ross, Sophia DeButts Gray and Patty Thum.

She was very active in the 1930s, showing in many of the Louisville Art Association exhibitions held at the Speed Art Museum. In one of those shows she entered a piece titled "Scene in Central Park, New York," but the catalog doesn't specify the medium. Schanzenbacher had added muralist and printmaker to her resume.

She lived in the family home on South Jackson Street and was known for haling in neighborhood children to paint their portraits. Failing eyesight forced her retirement in the late 1940s.

Landscape
lithograph
9 x 11 1/2 inches

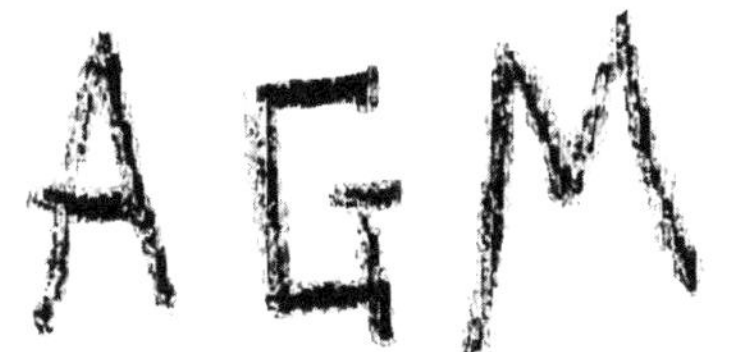

ALBERT GRAEME MITCHELL (1889-1941) was a Cincinnati, Ohio, physician who had drawn since childhood and was essentially a self-taught printmaker and painter.

Mitchell was a native of Salem, Massachusetts, and came to Cincinnati from Philadelphia, Pennsylvania. He was chairman of the pediatrics department at the University of Cincinnati College of Medicine and physician-in-chief at the Cincinnati Children's Hospital when the hospital underwent a major expansion with his leadership.

He wasn't the only doctor in the Queen City who had artistic tendencies. In the 1920s these men of medicine formed a society to exhibit their work. Among them were Josef Warkany, Thomas J. LeBlanc and Merlin L. Cooper. They had an etching show at Closson's Art Gallery in the 1930s.

Mitchell's memberships included the Cincinnati Crafters' Club, where he exhibited alongside E.T. Hurley, Arthur Helwig, Paul Ashbrook and Anita Fenton, and the Cincinnati Print and Drawing Circle. Mitchell collected prints, with a predilection for those caricaturing his profession. It is said that he wished to capture the vanishing views of Cincinnati in his art.

Spirits of the Ohio
drypoint
9 3/4 x 7 7/8 inches

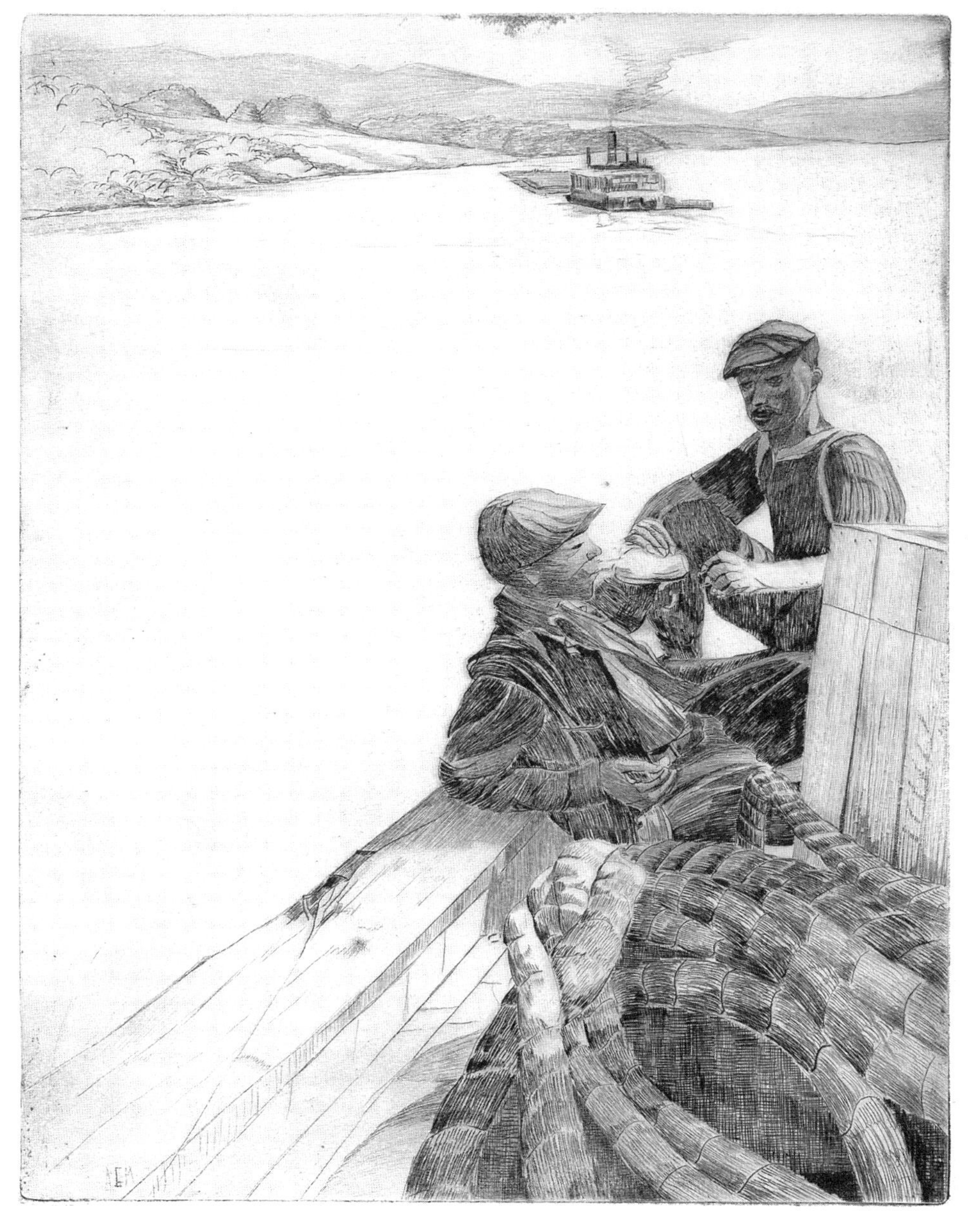

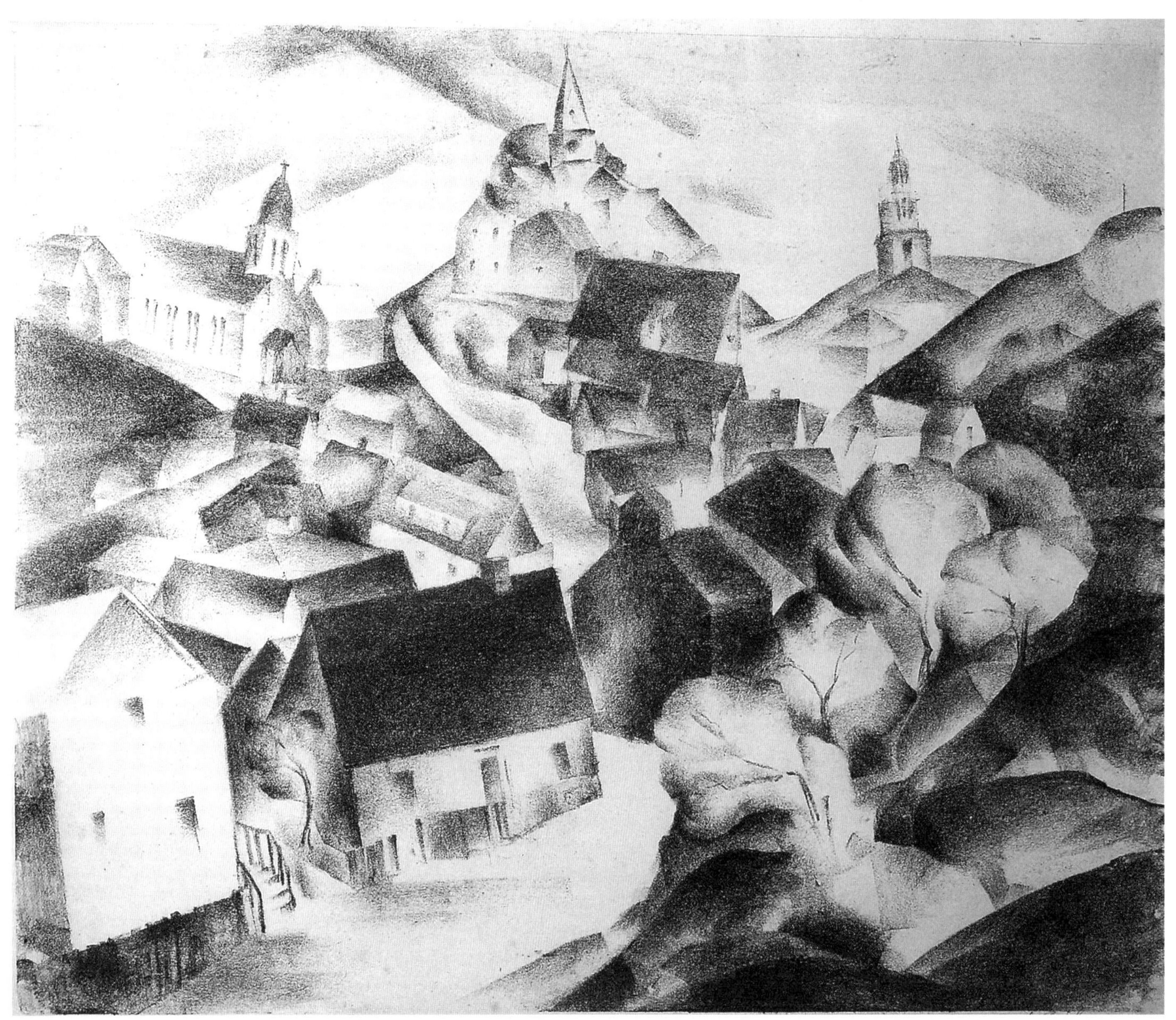

MAUD AINSLIE (1870-1960), a major force in the Louisville art world, is celebrated today as a printmaker. Her family had a summer home in Provincetown, Massachusetts, and Ainslie was involved in the art colony there for years, exhibiting with the Provincetown Art Association as early as 1917.

In 1915 Provincetown artists had started using a woodblock technique called white-line printmaking, and Ainslie took to it. In 1983 Ainslie was right there with all the other great printmakers such as Blanche Lazzell and Gustave Baumann in the *Provincetown Printers, A Woodcut Tradition* exhibition at the Smithsonian American Art Museum in Washington, D.C.

Ainslie helped establish the Louisville Art Association, the Louisville Handicraft Guild and the Louisville Art Center. In 1942 the Art Center merged with the Louisville Art Association, becoming the Art Center Association. She was an honorary life board member of that organization and served as president.

She painted modernist landscapes and still lifes, with a debt to Cezanne, Cubism and the American artists with whom she had studied, East-West fusionist Arthur Wesley Dow and Cubist William Zorach. She also worked in lithography.

Ainslie wasn't a frequent exhibitor considering the length of her career. She did shows at the Louisville Art Association in 1930, 1937 and 1940 and the Louisville Art Center in 1943 and 1954. In 1951 she had a one-woman show at the Hite Art Institute, University of Louisville, and in 2001 was included in the groundbreaking exhibition *Kentucky Women Artists: 1850-2000*, at the Owensboro (Kentucky) Museum of Fine Arts.

title unknown
lithograph
14 x 16 3/4 inches

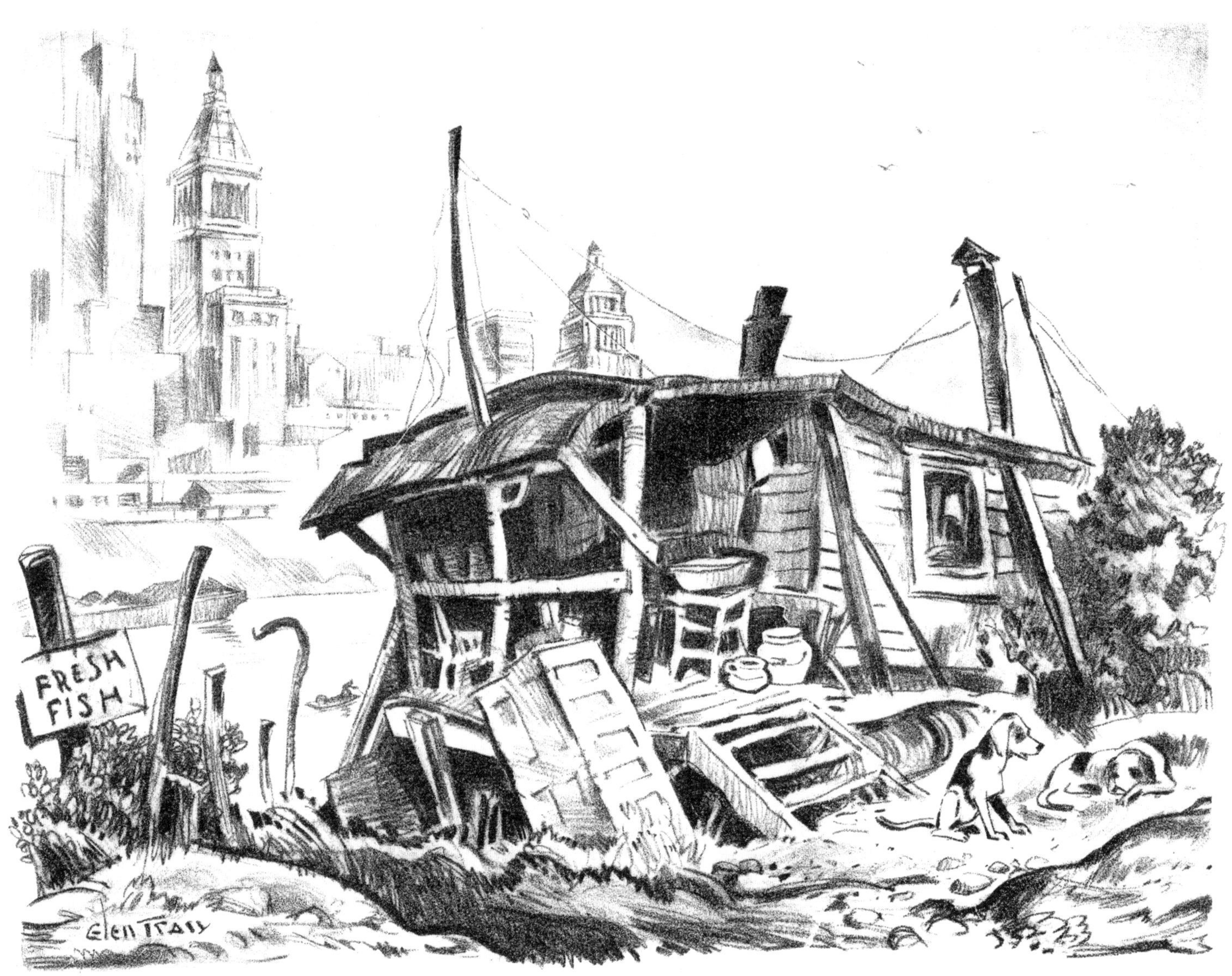
FRESH
FISH
Glen Tracy

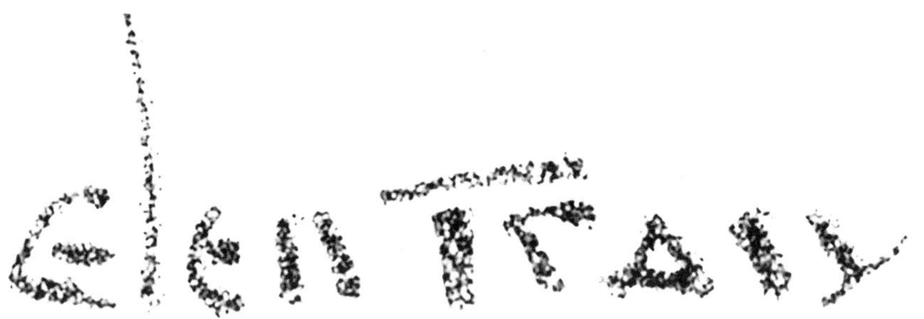

GLEN TRACY (1883-1956) was a Cincinnati, Ohio, artist known for his sympathetic depictions of urban life.

He attended the Art Academy of Cincinnati, studying under painter-etchers Frank Duveneck and Louis Henry Meakin, and taught there. He earned his living as a commercial artist and book illustrator. He exhibited for four decades, starting in the 1910s as a member of the Society of Western Artists. He depicted Cincinnati street life and life along the Ohio River, including the shanty-boat communities on both banks of the river.

Tracy became the poster boy for the peripatetic painter, traveling all over North America and capturing, for example, the Cumberland Falls area of Kentucky and the Smoky Mountains in Tennessee. He showed at the Corcoran Gallery of Art in Washington, D.C., the Scarab Club in Detroit, Michigan, and Closson's Art Gallery in Cincinnati. The latter advertised him as "one of Cincinnati's most distinguished artists." Tracy also exhibited in over 20 shows at the Cincinnati Art Museum.

Tracy had been "in a circus daze all his life," the *Cincinnati Enquirer* newspaper opined, and he followed the circus companies in a studio trailer. He spent his winters in Florida, where the circuses overwintered. Eventually, in 1951, he sold his New Richmond, Ohio, home and relocated to Sarasota, Florida.

Squatters Paradise
lithograph
7 x 9 1/4 inches

ROBERT GRIFFIN WATHEN (1910-1988) was a veteran of the Louisville, Kentucky, advertising world and pursued his fine-art interests in various media, including etching.

Speed Museum, Louisville Ky
drypoint
8 1/2 x 11 5/8 inches

The Madisonville, Kentucky, native received his art training in Louisville, at the Louisville School of Art and the Louisville Conservatory of Music. Alexander Van Leshout, the prime mover in a local etching revival, helped found the School of Art and, later, was the director of the art department at the conservatory. Wathen also studied with Paul Plaschke and Bethuel Moore, players in the regional art scene.

Wathen was the art director at the M.R. Kopmeyer Co. ad agency in Louisville, which was started in 1933, but left in the mid-1940s to establish a commercial art studio with Southern Indiana artist James J. Russell, son of regional art figure James L. Russell of New Albany. The younger Russell and Wathen were contemporaries, and Russell had studied with Plaschke and Moore.

Wathen also worked for the *Courier-Journal* and the Courier-Journal Job Printing Co. He was known to carry his watercolor box all over the area, capturing images for his "Our Town" series in the newspaper and for color-gravure features in the paper's *Sunday Magazine*. These features included "Louisville Bridges," Gray Street, Second Street, Lexington Road and the St. James Court Art Show. He also illustrated the syndicated feature "You Be the Judge."

The artist had several exhibitions, including those at the Louisville Art Center in 1944, the Speed Art Museum in 1949 and the Spalding University gallery in 1965. He was a member of the Louisville Watercolor Society and the Ad Club. He taught at the Southeastern Art Center in Jeffersonville starting in 1945.

When Wathen took up etching, his daughter, Fran Delaney, related, he would work at home with the children watching from a safe distance. Eventually the artist established a studio in downtown Louisville and that danger passed.

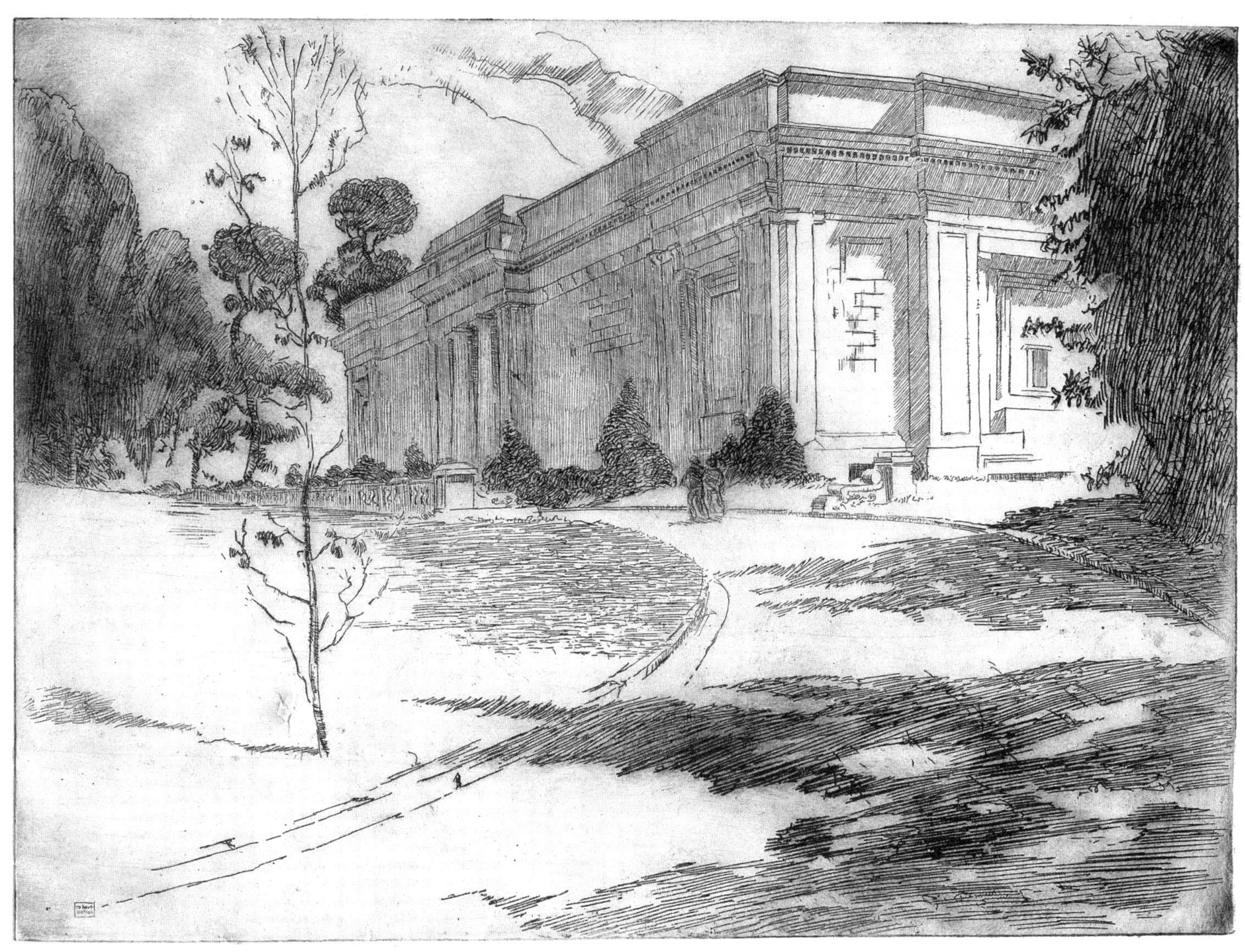

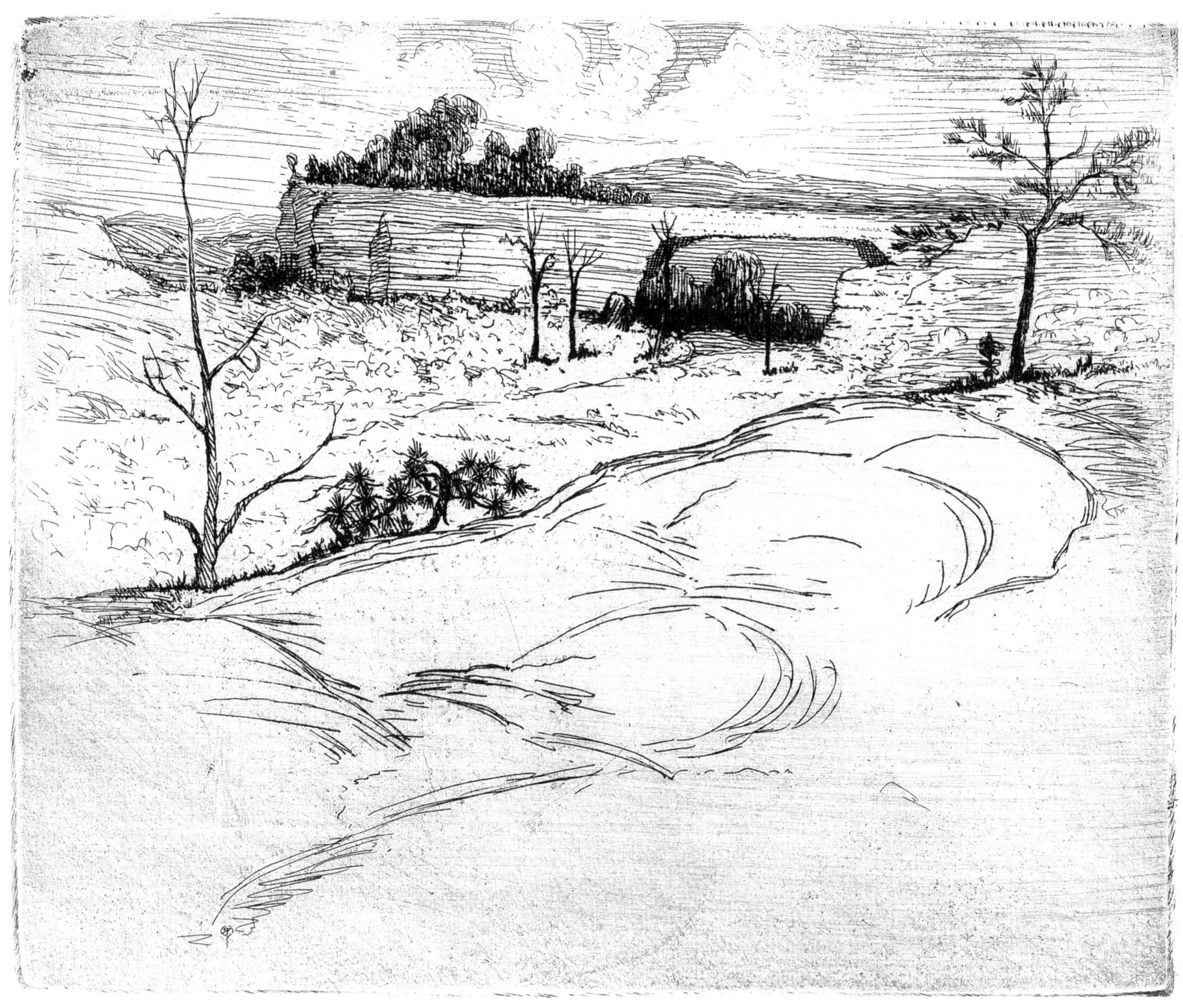

Frank G Robbins

In 1941 Louisville artist **FRANK GARDNER ROBBINS** was asked to reproduce a rare John J. Audubon watercolor of a Kentucky cardinal. The request came from a Galt House heir who wanted copies for members of her family. Robbins etched the image in copper, printed 50 copies on his own press and hand-colored them.

Robbins (1886-1952) had been etching for decades. He was the president of the Robbins-Pope Engraving Co. and had described himself as a steel- and copper-plate engraver in his World War I draft-registration form. His *Courier-Journal* obituary identified him as a portrait and landscape painter, which was true enough but overlooked his track record as a fine-art etcher of scenes in Kentucky and Tennessee – and of Audubon watercolors.

As early as 1912 this graduate of the School of the Art Institute of Chicago was exhibiting with such Kentucky art heavy hitters as Harvey Joiner, Carl Brenner, Robert Burns Wilson and Enid Yandell in the Kentucky Traveling Art Gallery sponsored by the Kentucky Federation of Women's Clubs. In 1919 he was in a Composition and Sketch Club of Louisville exhibition.

Throughout the 1930s he showed in the Louisville Artists League's *Kentucky and Southern Indiana Artists Exhibitions* at the Speed Art Museum. In 1932 Robbins showed 20 pieces in the *First Exhibition of Paintings and Sketches by the Louisville Sketch Club* at the Speed. Among them were *Natural Bridge State Park*, *Old Kentucky Home* and *Umbrella Rock*. The exhibition showcased drawings, paintings – and etchings.

He maintained a studio in a downtown commercial building and was a member of the Arts Club. By 1950 he was helping run a St. Matthews community art festival and was advertising as a "cleaner and repairer" of oil paintings and frames.

As for the Audubon print, those that didn't go to the heir were sold. One was presented to the curator of ornithology at the Museum of Natural History in New York City, another went to the Audubon Society in Henderson, Kentucky, and four were given to the Speed. The watercolor is in the collection of the Filson Historical Society.

Natural Bridge State Park
etching
1932
6 x 7 1/2 inches

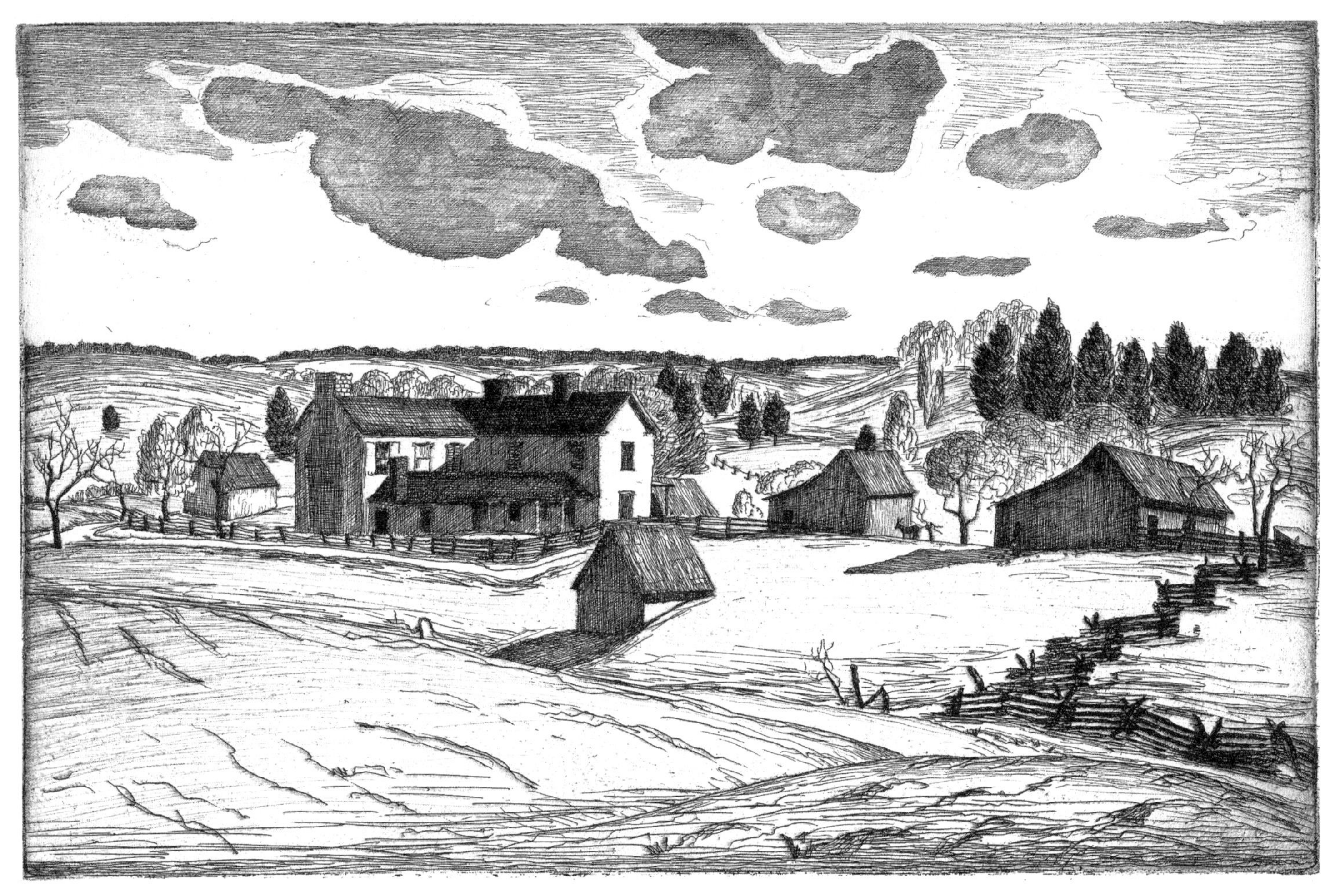

Beatrice S. Levy

BEATRICE SOPHIA LEVY (1892-1974) was an important Chicago, Illinois, artist with deep connections to Kentucky.

She was a member of the German immigrant Levy family best known in Louisville for the Levy Bros. department store. The Levy business had its beginnings in Harrodsburg, and the artist's mother, the former Sarah Steinfeld, was born in Paris, Kentucky, and was married in Louisville. The artist told Chicago art critic C.J. Bulliet that she had adopted Kentucky as her "painter's paradise" on visits there.

Levy was a Chicago native and a graduate of the School of the Art Institute of Chicago. She did further study at the artist colony of Provincetown, Massachusetts, where she mastered the colored-aquatint technique, and in New York City. Though she exhibited as early as 1915 at the Panama-Pacific International Exhibition in San Francisco, California, her heyday came during the WPA or American Scene era of the 1930s. She showed at the 1933 Century of Progress Exposition in Chicago and the 1939 New York World's Fair. She served as the supervisor of the Federal Art Gallery, part of the New Deal economic push, in 1936 in Chicago and was an officer with the Chicago Society of Etchers and the Chicago Society of Artists. In the 1950s she relocated to La Jolla, California.

Her works are in the Art Institute, Smithsonian American Art Museum and the Library of Congress, Washington, D.C., Los Angeles County Museum of Art and Bibliotheque nationale de France.

In Bulliet's 1936 Levy profile, part of his "Artists of Chicago Past and Present" series in the *Chicago Daily News*, he wrote: "The hills and fields and types of people around Harrodsburg have furnished motifs for her very real contributions to 'the American scene,' in both paint and etchers' ink." There are at least four Kentucky etchings – *On a Kentucky Road; Duncan, Kentucky; Front Porch, Harrodsburg;* and *Farm at Bohon* – and at least one Kentucky painting, *A Street I Remember*.

Farm at Bohon, Kentucky
etching
1932
7 x 10 7/8 inches

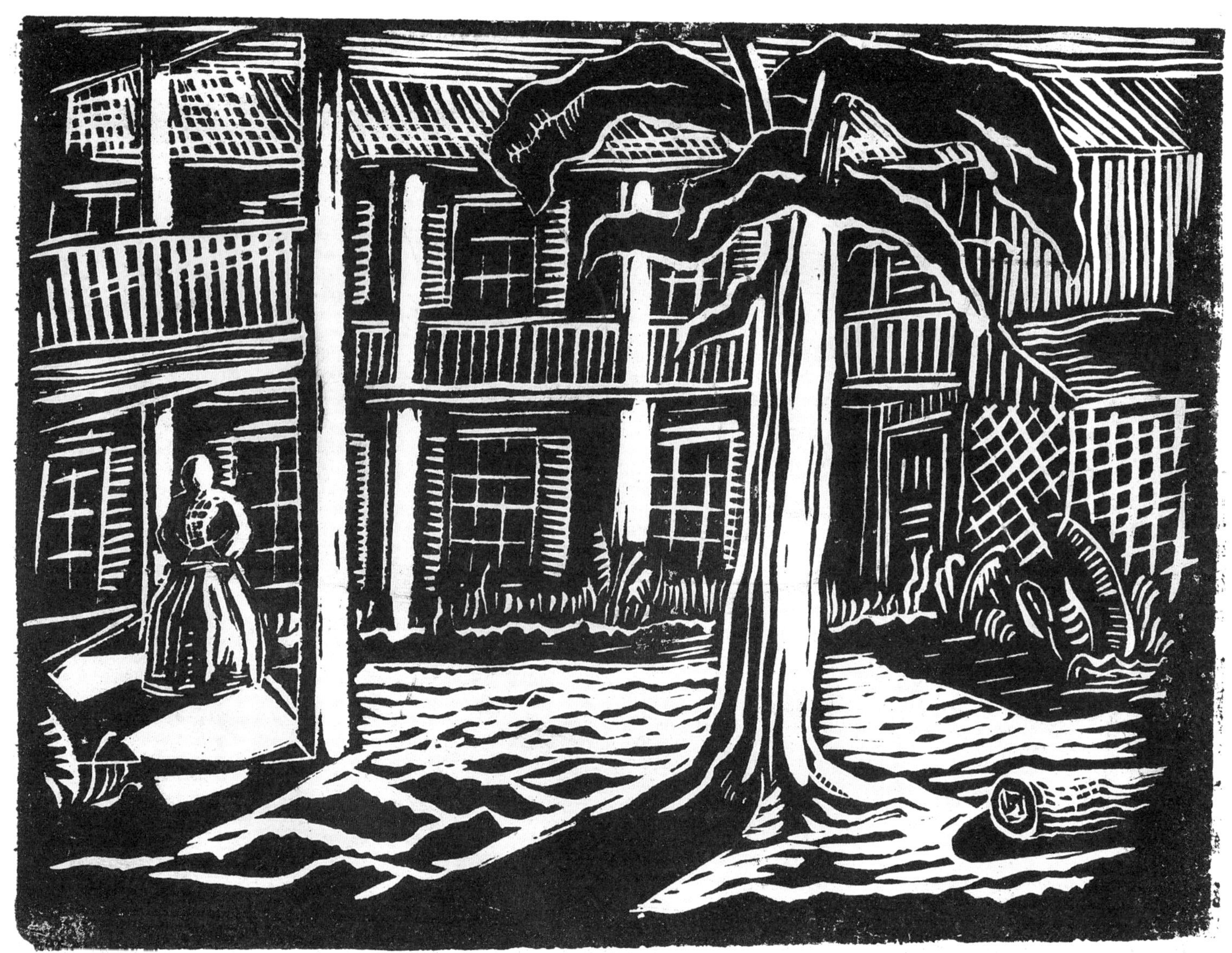

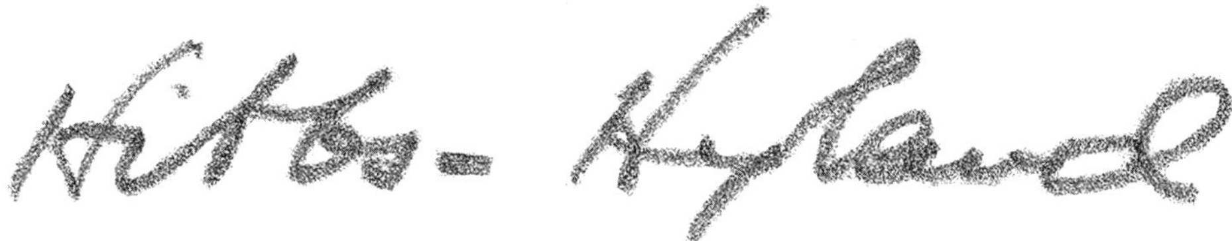

RUTH HIBBS HYLAND (1906-1983) was raised in Smithland, Kentucky, and had a career in art education.

She attended the University of Illinois at Urbana-Champaign, where she met Frederick T. Hyland, an architecture student. They married in Smithland in 1935. A year later they moved to Richmond, Virginia, where Mrs. Hyland's brother, Henry, ran the Richmond Professional Institute (Virginia Commonwealth Institute). She taught there, founding the art education department, and the school offers a scholarship in her name. She also served a stint as the director of art education for the Richmond Public Schools.

Her husband became one of the leading Richmond exponents of the Modern style in architecture in the 1950s and 1960s. They had both apprenticed with Frank Lloyd Wright.

In the late 1960s, Mrs. Hyland fell ill and would be hospitalized until her death.

Information is non-existent about her endeavors in art, not just art education. An article on Smithland history in the *Paducah Sun* in 1950 at least helps date the "*Clark House" Smithland Ky.* lithograph. The Clark House was a "popular pioneer inn, which cracked and collapsed after the flood of 1937." The 1930s were a time of interest in portraying historic American scenes in art, and block prints were a popular medium to do just that.

"Clark House" Smithland, Ky.
block print
1934
6 3/8 x 8 1/2 inches

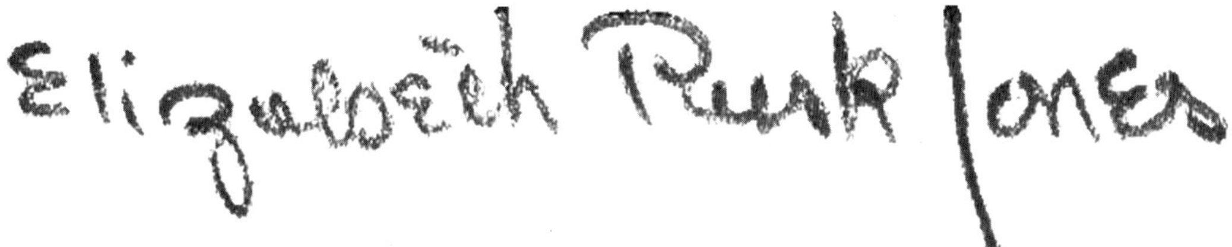

ELIZABETH RUSK JONES GREENHALL (1915-2002) was a native of New York City. She was a graduate of Barnard College and Teachers College, Columbia University. She was a teacher in the New Jersey Public Schools.

Her father was Wilfred J. Jones, a celebrated book illustrator who had an interest in block printing. That and a family trip to Paris, France, cemented her interest in art.

She married zoologist Arthur M. Greenhall in 1942 and moved to Portland, Oregon, where he had accepted the job of curator of the Portland Zoo (Oregon Zoo). Another zoo position presented itself, this at the Detroit Zoo, and the family moved to Michigan.

Arthur Greenhall's interest in the Tropics and vampire bats took the family to Trinidad in the 1950s. Mrs. Greenhall was quite active in the Art Society of Trinidad and Tobago. She had always been interested in sculpture, and the clays of the island fascinated her. She designed an exhibit showing how archaic stones found on the island were used to work clay. The Greenhalls returned to the United States in 1963.

The etching on the facing page was found with another and attributed to Louisville, Kentucky, artist and ceramicist Mary Alice Hadley though it was signed by Mrs. Greenhall. The prints may have been part of the Hadley estate. In 1936 Hadley was an art student at Columbia University while her husband pursued a degree. It seems probable that the two women knew each other, shared an interest in art and ceramics, and that's how two etchings by Elizabeth Rusk Jones Greenhall turned up in Louisville linked to Mary Alice Hadley.

title unknown
etching
undated, circa 1936
7 x 4 7/8 inches

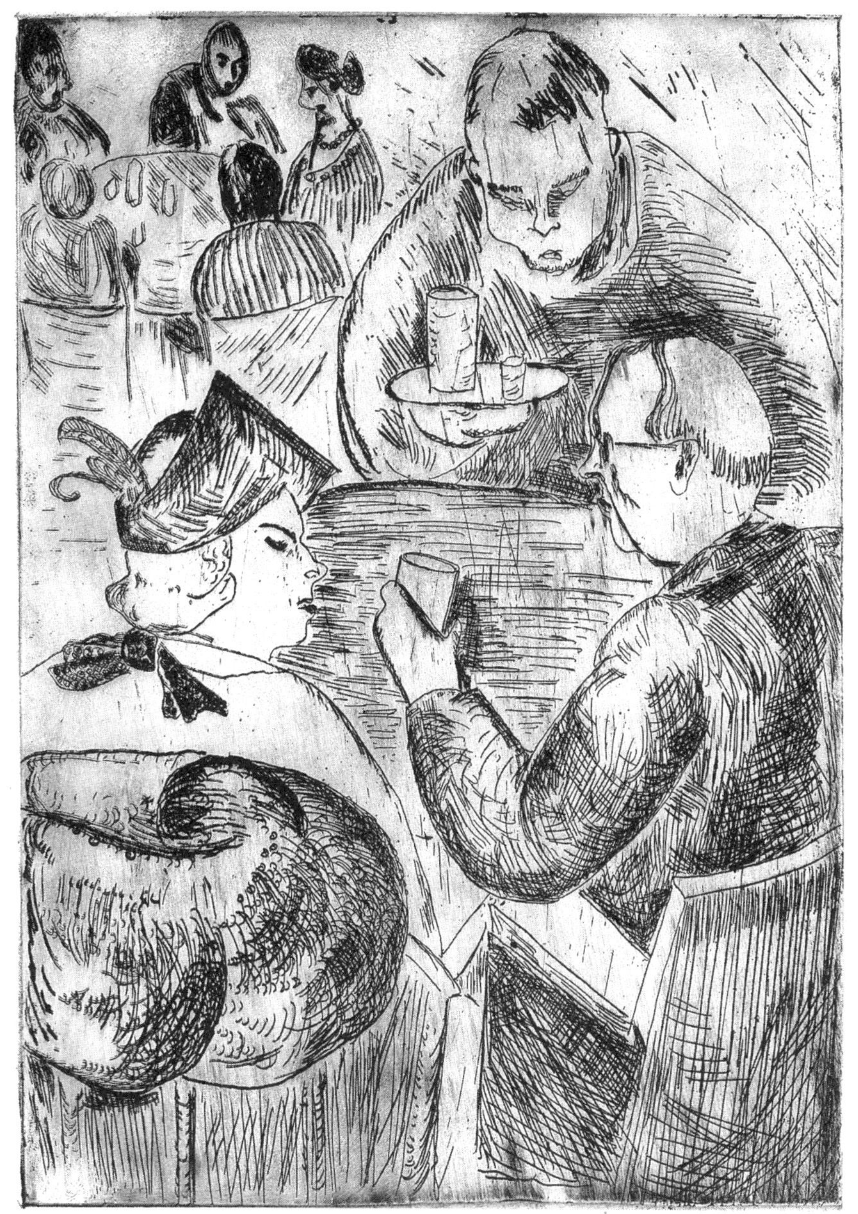

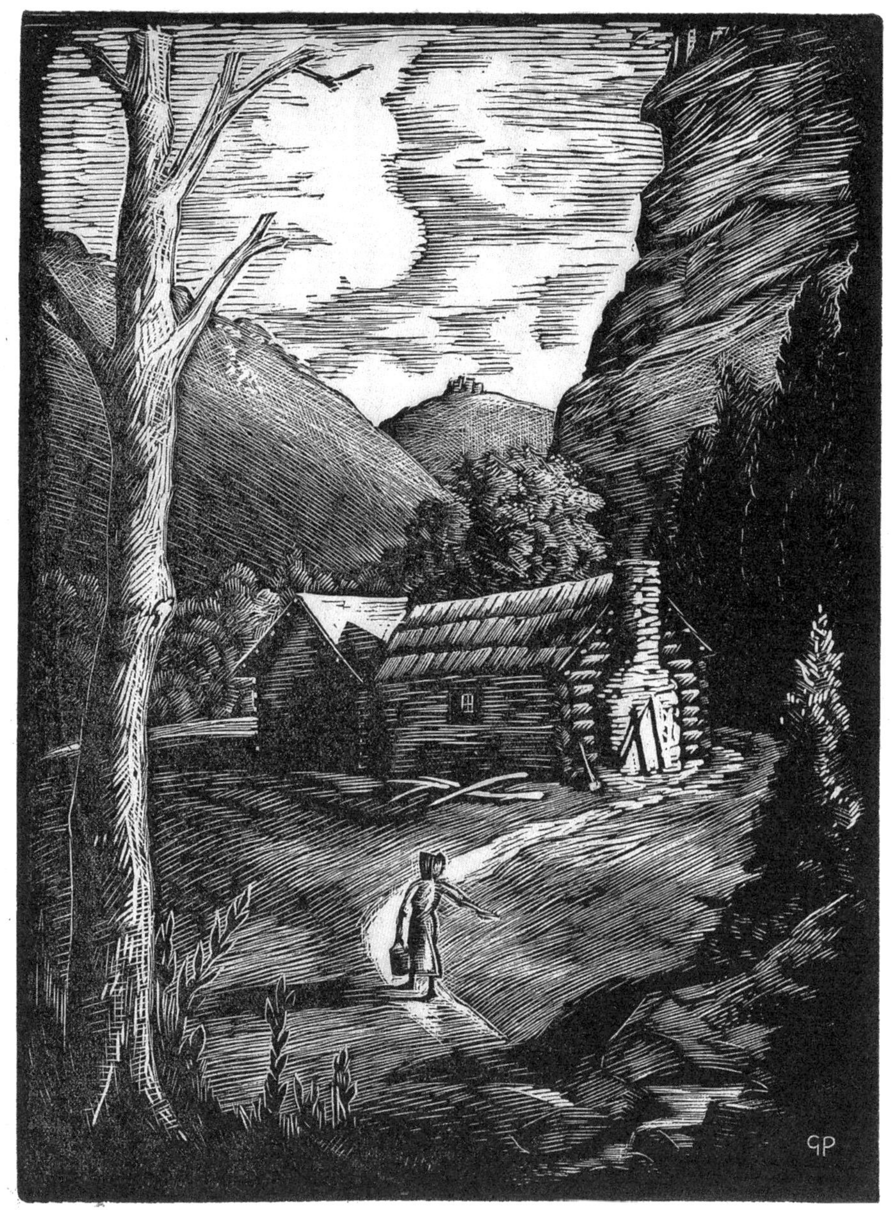

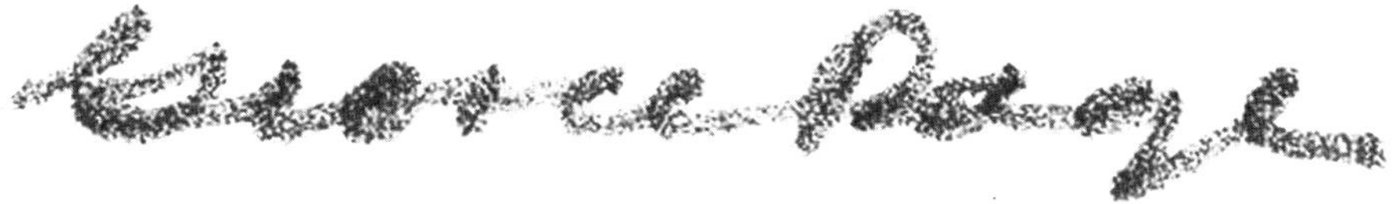

The Rockcastle Country
block print
edition 5/50
1936
8 x 6 inches

GROVER PAGE (1892-1958) was a North Carolina native who came to Louisville, Kentucky, in 1919 to work for the *Courier-Journal* newspaper as an editorial cartoonist, a post he held until 1956.

Page studied at the School of the Art Institute of Chicago with such fellow cartoonists as Billy Debeck, creator of *Barney Google*, and Frank King, of *Gasoline Alley* fame. After a stint as a mechanical engineer in his hometown of Gastonia, Page nabbed the political cartoonist position at the *Tennessean* newspaper in Nashville in 1917.

Two years later, Page was working in Louisville and living across the Ohio River in New Albany, Indiana. He became a significant participant in the vigorous art scene in New Albany. He was a charter member of the Wonderland Way Art Club there and exhibited in the first Wonderland Way show in 1935.

GP

As celebrated as Page was for his newspaper cartooning, he was also well-known for his block prints. His *Noah*, also known as *Ohio River Noah*, took the first prize in the 1940 Southern States Art League printmaker competition. Prints from his nostalgic newspaper series *Horse & Buggy Days* were reproduced in the *American Block Print Calendar* of 1939 and in a 1942 calendar put out by the Wood Mosaic Co. of Louisville. Page, the company touted, used Wood-Mosaic end-grain maple blocks for his prints.

The printmaker exhibited mainly in the Midwest and South. The cartoonist exhibited in the 1951 National Society of Cartoonists show at the Metropolitan Museum of Art in New York City.

The Carnegie Center for Art & History in New Albany had an exhibition for Page and his artist son in 2000, *From the Headlines to the Frontlines: The Artwork of Grover Page and Grover Page Jr.*

The Rockcastle Country, opposite, was shown in the *Second Annual Exhibit of the Wonderland Way Art Club* in New Albany in 1936.

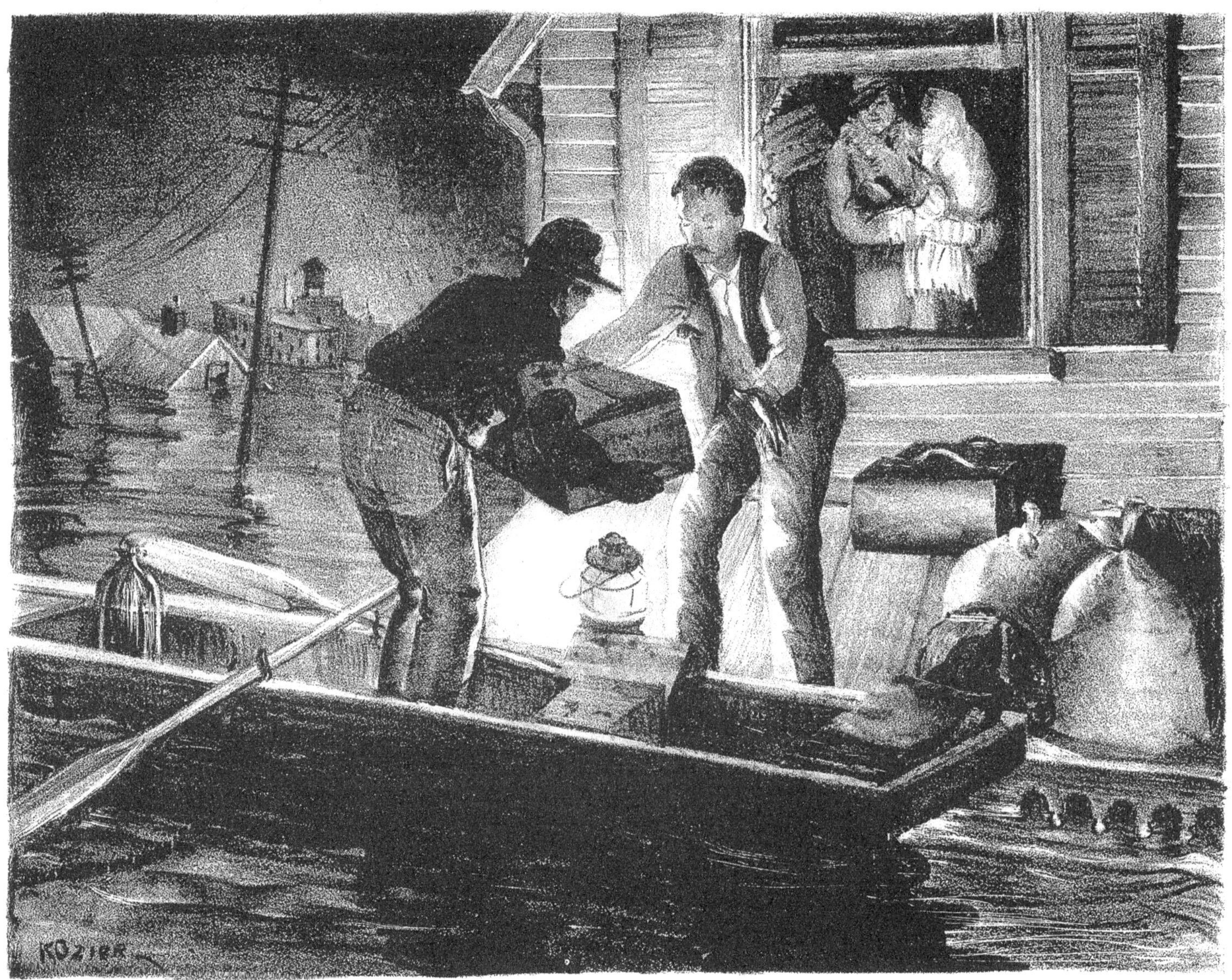
KOZIER

Kenneth Ozier

KENNETH W. OZIER was a Cincinnati, Ohio, painter, printmaker and illustrator.

Ozier (1905-1978) received his training at the Art Academy of Cincinnati, the Pennsylvania Academy of the Fine Arts in Philadelphia, the University of Cincinnati, George Washington University in Washington, D.C., and the Ohio Mechanics Institute in Cincinnati. He studied fine art, advertising layout and design and medical illustration.

He earned his living as a freelancer in advertising art and illustration until the outbreak of World War II. He worked for the U.S. Navy in Washington and then for Washington newspapers as a layout artist and photo retoucher. He returned to Cincinnati in the late 1940s, again freelancing.

Ozier was a charter member of the Professional Artists of Cincinnati. He belonged to two other Cincinnati art organizations, the Men's Art Club and the Cincinnati Crafters' Club. He was a member of the Print Council of America.

His printmaking seems to have been concentrated in the 1930s during the American Regionalist movement. Two of his lithographs, *Refugees, 1937*, and *Shanty Boat in Winter,* were honored at their respective exhibitions, in Pennsylvania and in Washington, D.C. He continued to exhibit through the early 1960s.

His works are held by the Public Library of Cincinnati and Hamilton County and the University of Cincinnati. His *Old Kentucky Home* etching is in the collection of the My Old Kentucky Home State Park in Bardstown, Kentucky.

title unknown
lithograph
1937
6 x 7 3/4 inches

Howard Simon

In the 1930s New York artist **HOWARD SIMON** (1902-1979) created a series of woodcuts celebrating great American composers. Included was the "father of American music," Stephen Collins Foster, composer of "My Old Kentucky Home, Good-Night!"

The 1930s were a time of economic and political turmoil, and the art movement then peaking was American Regionalism. Scenes of Americana were celebrated, creating in many a national pride despite the hard times. Simon was part of that movement.

Simon was born in New York City and received some art training there but left for Paris, France, while a teenager. He attended the Academie Julian and learned how to make woodblock prints from Japanese artists. He returned from Europe in the late 1920s and took up residence in San Francisco, California. He was a member of the California Society of Etchers and other local arts groups.

Simon's writer wife, the former Charlie May Hogue, was a native of Arkansas and wanted to return to her home state to live a more back-to-nature existence. The couple moved in 1930, built a log cabin and bartered for whatever they needed, with Simon dividing his time between the homestead and New York. Simon was well on his way to becoming a well-known printmaker, painter and book illustrator. The Arkansas idyll lasted five years, ending in divorce.

Simon continued his art career and taught, serving on the art faculty of New York University for 24 years and spending his latter years as chairman of the art department at the Barlow School in upstate New York. He also wrote what one reviewer has described as the "unrivaled treasury of the methods, techniques, and examples of the great illustrators," *500 Years of Art in Illustration,* published in 1942.

Very Respectfully Yours Stephen C. Foster
block print
1938
11 x 9 inches

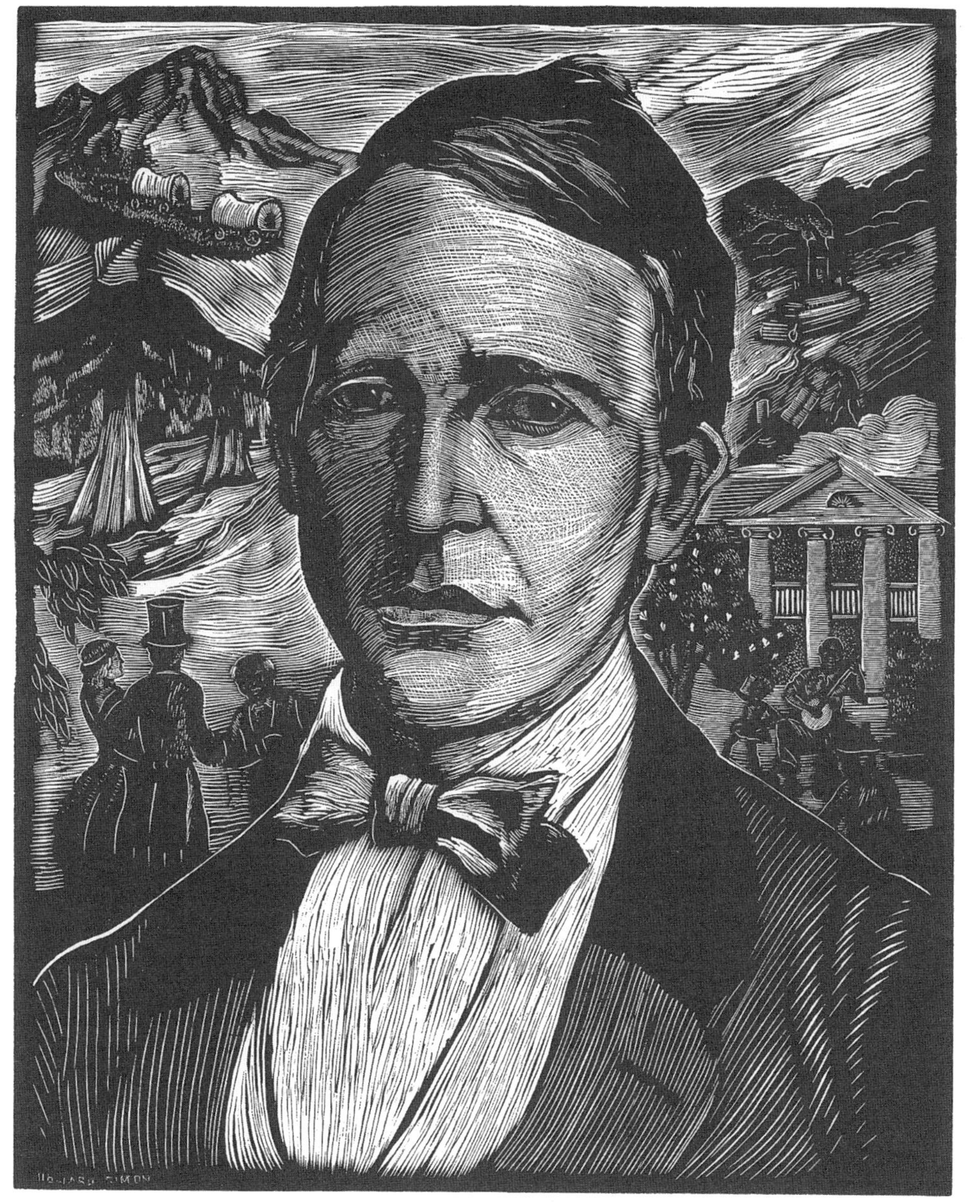

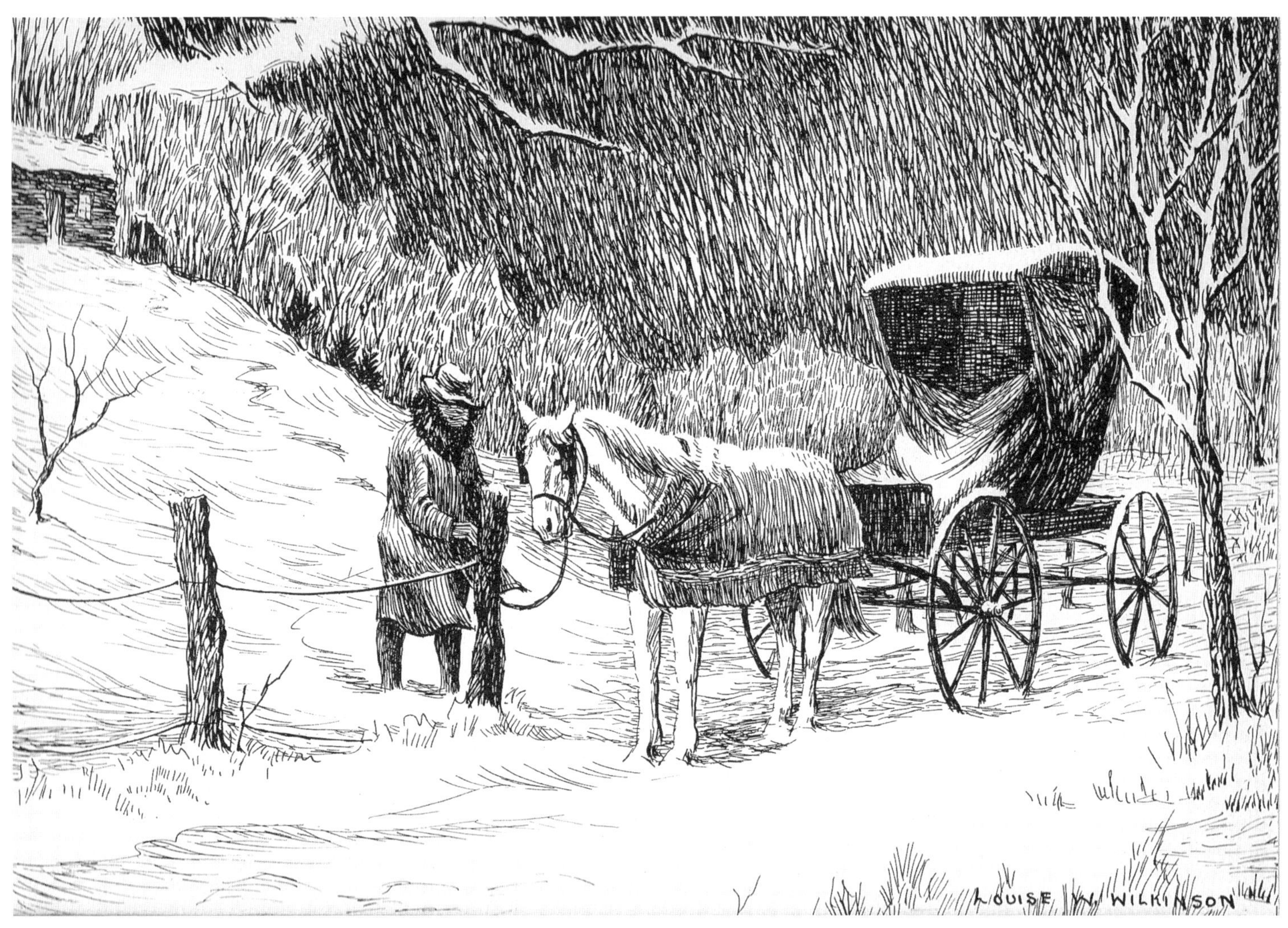
LOUISE W. WILKINSON

LOUISE W. WILKINSON

title unknown
offset lithograph
6 1/4 x 8 7/8 inches (sight)

LOUISE WILKINSON (1899-1984) was a successful genre painter who worked in both Kentucky and Indiana. She lived in Danville, Kentucky, and was a member of the legendary Brown County Art Gallery Association in Nashville, Indiana.

She was "a painter of rural and small-town Kentucky," Jack Kellam, the late Centre College art professor, said in a 1984 newspaper article, adding, "That's what she loves." She also had a "tremendous love of animals … evident on many a canvas," as noted in her profile in the 1971 publication *Brown County Art and Artists*.

Mrs. Wilkinson was a native of Harrodsburg, Kentucky, studied at the Kentucky College for Women in Danville and was associated with Centre. She also received instruction from the American Academy of Art in Chicago, Illinois, and the Art Instruction Schools of Minneapolis, Minnesota.

The artist exhibited all over the United States, even at Gimbels department store in New York City. In addition to the Brown County group, her memberships included the Kentucky Guild of Artists and Craftsmen, Lexington (Kentucky) Art League, Wind River Art Guild in Wyoming, Louisville (Kentucky) Art Center and Wilderness Trace Arts League.

She was well-known for her pen-and-inks of historic sites in Kentucky, especially the McDowell House in Danville and Liberty Hall in Frankfort, many of those views being made into note cards. She also sold offset prints of her more popular paintings and hand-blocked Christmas cards.

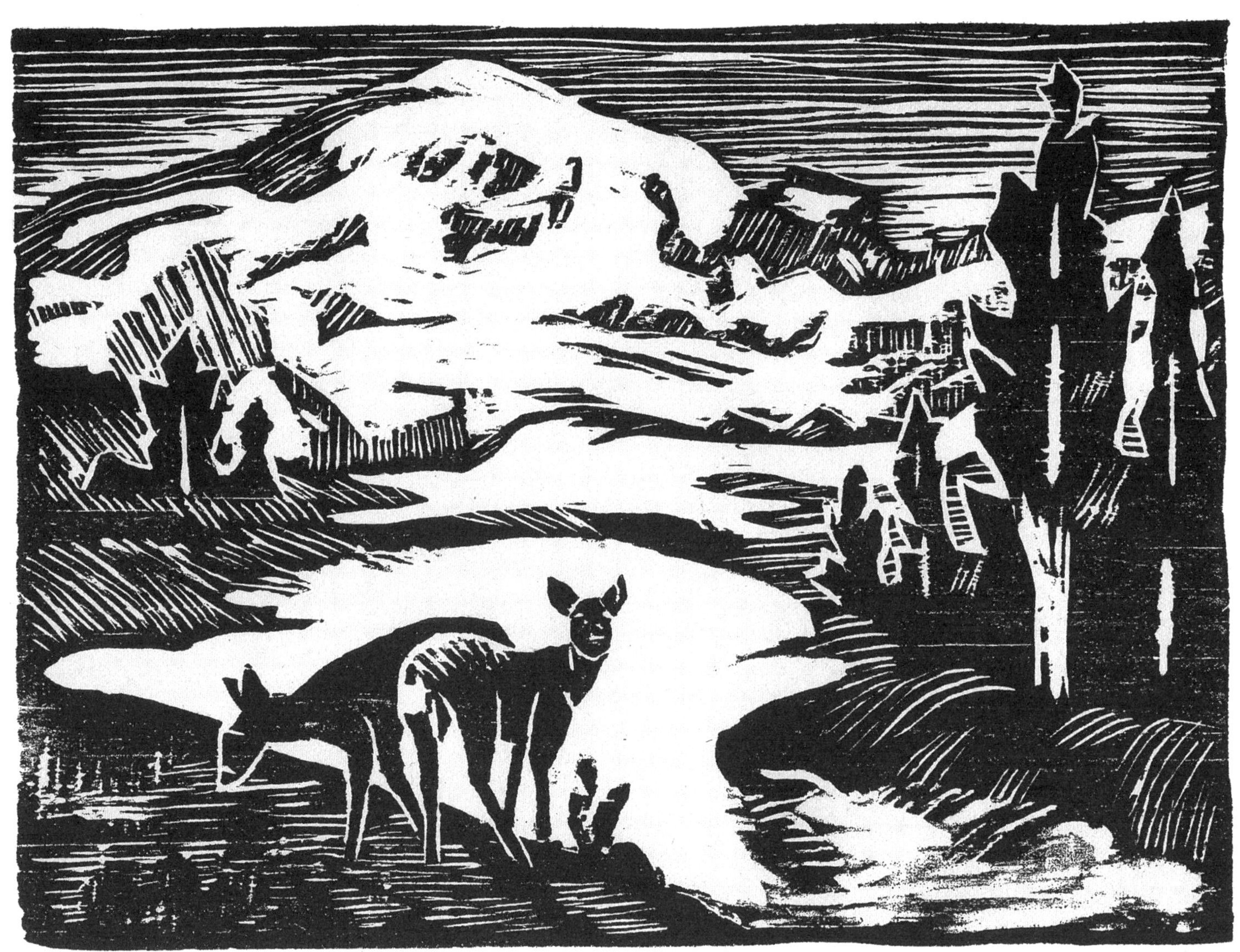

E. Sophonisba Hergesheimer

ELLA SOPHONISBA HERGESHEIMER (1873-1943) was a Nashville, Tennessee, artist who figured prominently in the art scene of Bowling Green, Kentucky.

Hergesheimer was a native of Allentown, Pennsylvania, and a descendant of landmark American painter Charles Willson Peale. She studied at the Pennsylvania Academy of the Fine Arts in Philadelphia and in Europe. Among her teachers were portraitist Cecilia Beaux, Impressionist William Merritt Chase and printmaker Blanche Lazzell.

She came to Nashville, Tennessee, to paint a portrait and never left. "She captivated the South and was in turn captivated by it" is how a 1912 *Harper's Bazaar* article put it. She was an important part of the artistic ferment in the Nashville of the 1920s and 1930s. She executed many portraits of Tennessee and Kentucky notables, including women's rights advocate Madeline McDowell Breckinridge of Lexington, Kentucky. She was also known for her still lifes and for "fine lithographs and color wood blocks," according to a 1957 article in the *Tennessean* newspaper. She exhibited in such cities as Lexington, Philadelphia, Cincinnati, Ohio, and Asheville, North Carolina.

Hergesheimer taught art, having a class in her studio at least once a week. In 1923 she told the *Morning Call* newspaper of Allentown, Pennsylvania, "I just love to teach, especially when I feel that I am really opening the eyes of my pupils to seeing some of the wonderful beauty around them."

Her classes in Bowling Green were very influential, and her circle there included artists Frances Herrick Fowler, Sarah Gaines Peyton and Wickliffe Cooper Covington. In 1925 she exhibited a painting titled *Bowling Green after the Storm.*

Her *Mount Rainier* print is from the 1939 *American Block Print Calendar* published by the Gutenberg Publishing Co. of Chicago, Illinois.

Mount Rainier
block print
1939
4 1/2 x 6 1/8 inches

JOHN ADAMS SPELMAN III (1912-1969) was a Minnesota native who expressed his deep connection to Appalachia in block prints of mountain life.

Spelman came South in the mid-1930s to teach art at the old Asheville Farm School in the Swannanoa Valley, near Asheville, North Carolina. While there he came into contact with the artists at the nearby Black Mountain College, a hotbed of experimental art, music and architecture.

He moved to Kentucky to work at the Pine Mountain Settlement School in Harlan County from 1938 to 1941 as art instructor, houseparent and artist-in-residence. He also was a staff artist for the *Mountain Life & Work* magazine published by the Council of the Southern Mountains.

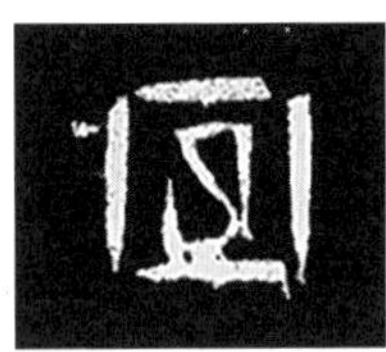

Spelman's prints, which appeared in Pine Mountain school calendars and publications, were collected in a 1939 book, *At Home in the Hills: Glimpses of Harlan County, Kentucky, Through the Media of Linoleum Block and the Woodcut,* printed by the Pine Mountain Print Shop.

He writes in the book's preface that "the whole purpose of this collection is to show by line and mass the simple beauty of the mountain home, even in its state of dilapidation. … Where else can one find houses that so grow out of the soil, chimneys with so much unconscious beauty in their lines, roofs and wall spaces with such 'at-oneness'?"

Spelman was greatly influenced by his father, John A. Spelman II, an outdoorsman and member of the Chicago, Illinois, art scene known for his paintings of the Smoky Mountains. The father died in 1941, and the junior Spelman returned to Minnesota.

Deserted Cabin
block print
1939
6 x 7 inches

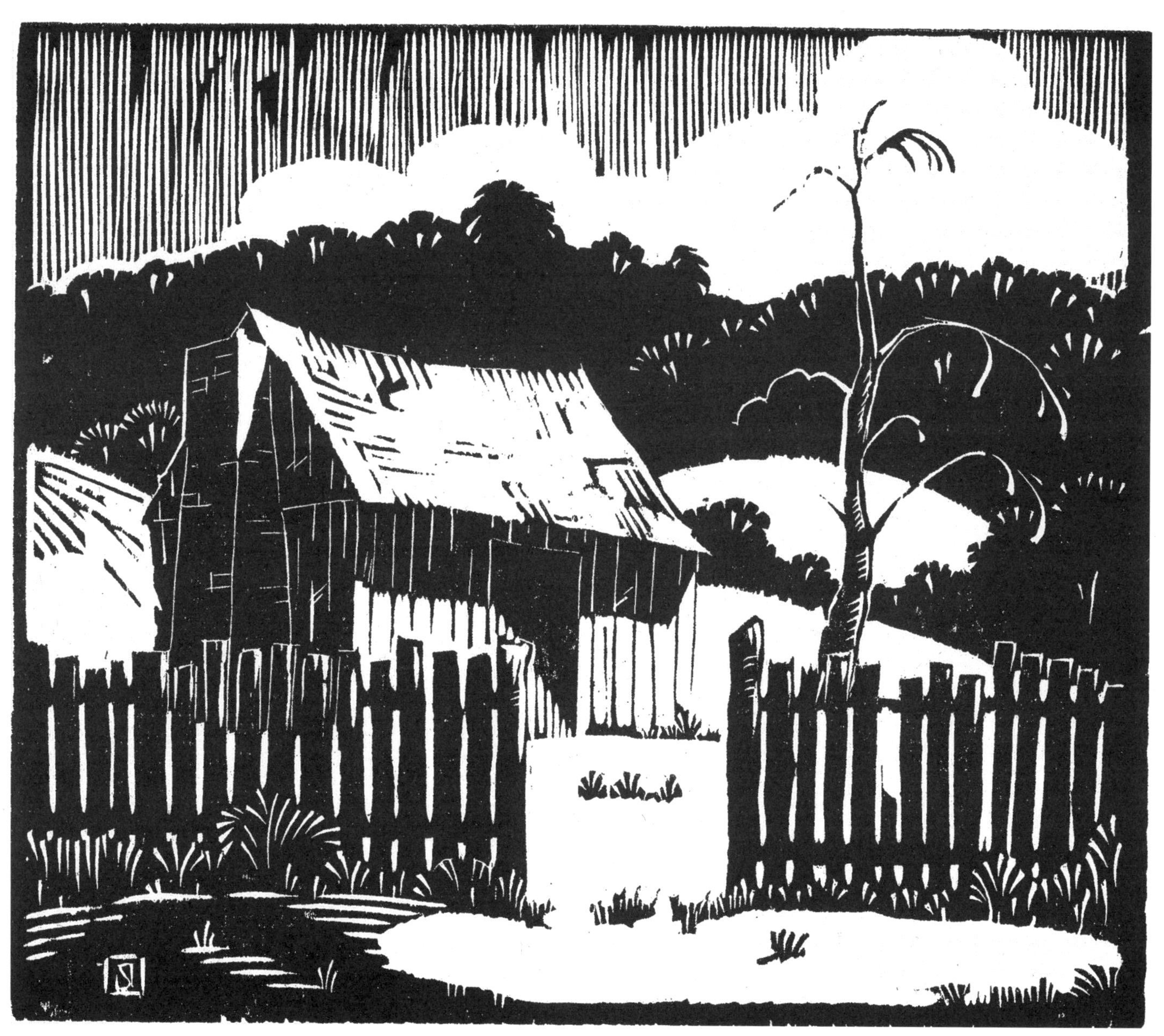

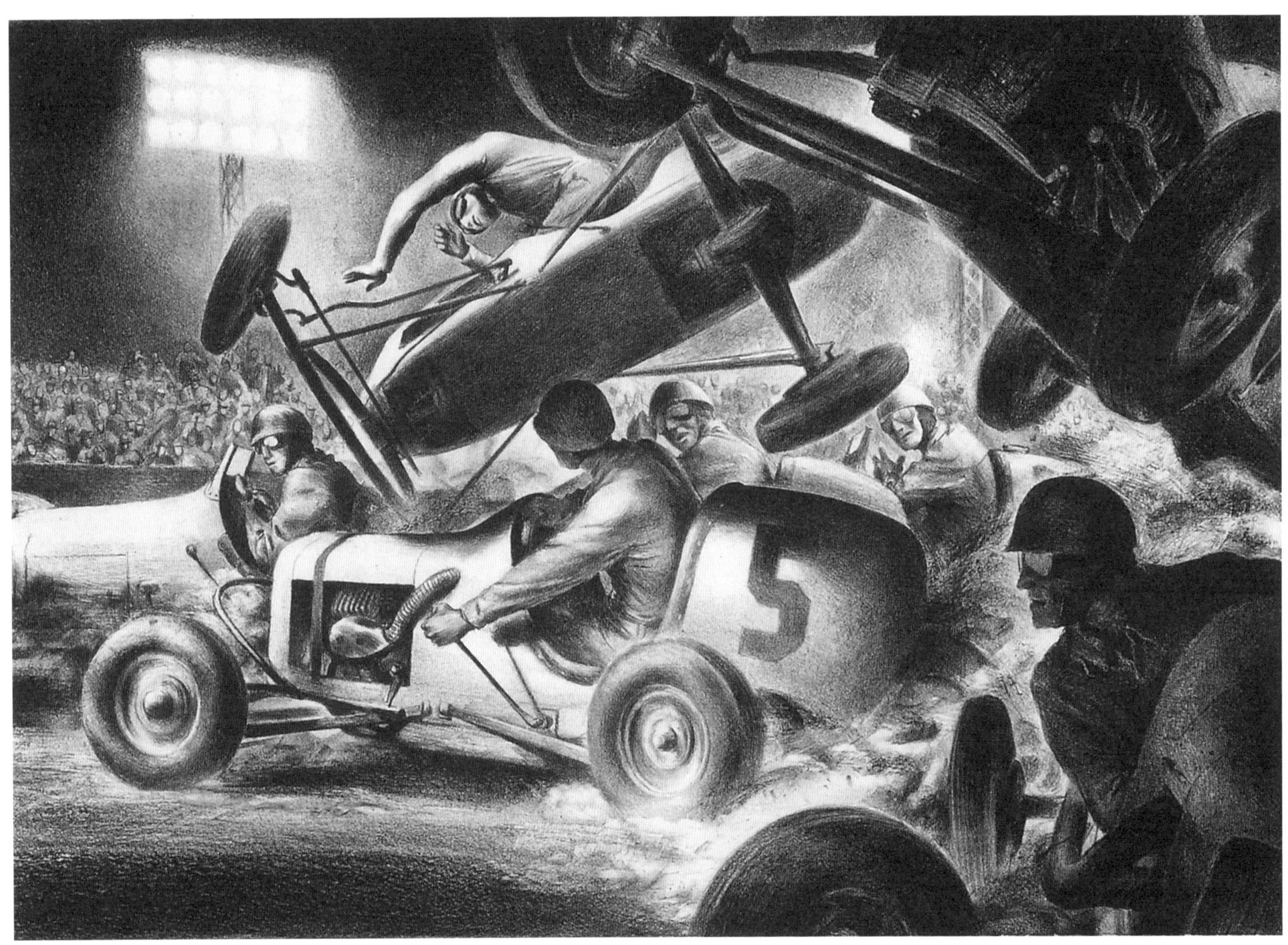

Paul E. Nonnast

Illustrator and graphic designer **PAUL NONNAST** (1918-1993) came to Kentucky late in his life. The Carlisle, Pennsylvania, native had trained at the Philadelphia Museum and School of Industrial Art and worked in a lithography shop. In the 1940s he was a staff artist for the *Philadelphia Record*, taught at the Moore Institute of Art, Science and Industry in Philadelphia and freelanced.

His commercial art career spanned the mid-20th century. His illustrations appeared in the *Saturday Evening Post*, *Reader's Digest*, *Woman's Day*, *Cosmopolitan* and *Field & Stream*. He did advertising work for Bell Telephone, Chevrolet and United Airlines.

He moved to Kentucky in 1988. He had worked with *Concern* magazine, a Presbyterian Women publication, in New York City. When the Presbyterian Church (U.S.A.) moved its headquarters to Louisville, Nonnast came along and served as art consultant to *Horizons*, the renamed magazine. He retired in 1993.

In 1945 a piece of his was included in the exhibition *Modern Art in Advertising: An Exhibition of Designs for Container Corporation of America* at the Art Institute of Chicago. The exhibition traveled throughout the country and was documented in two catalogs. Nonnast shared wall space with Dean Cornwell, a Louisville native.

The Presbyterian Center in Louisville had a retrospective of his work in the 1990s. He was in a 2013 exhibition *Paintings by American Illustrators* at Central Connecticut State University. It consisted of paintings from the Sanford Low Collection of Illustration at the New Britain Museum of American Art. And he is in the Smithsonian American Art Museum collection in Washington, D.C.

Nonnast's work in lithography is not well-documented. In 1939 he is known to have shown *For Want of a Horse* in a Philadelphia Print Club show. According to a Presbyterian Church article, the artist's remaining work, most of it done early in his career, was distributed in the early 2000s to institutions that house collections of commercial art.

title unknown
lithograph
10 x 14 1/2 inches

C. Cregor Reid

CELIA CREGOR REID (1895-1956) was a Kentucky native who became an integral member of the St. Augustine, Florida, art colony in the first half of the 20th century.

Fatio House
block print
9 1/4 x 8 1/8 inches

She was born in Springfield and was a graduate of the University of Kentucky. She furthered her art training at the School of the Art Institute of Chicago, the Carnegie Institute in Pittsburgh, Pennsylvania, and the Maryland Institute College of Art in Baltimore.

She relocated to St. Augustine in 1926 and joined the Galleon Club, described as a group of wintering artists and writers. In 1936 the St. Augustine Arts Club was founded, absorbing the Galleon Club. As word got out about the club, artists from New England, Chicago and Cincinnati, Ohio, showed up and became part of the burgeoning art colony. Reid was a supporter of the club and the city.

C·CREGOR ·REID·

Reid's linocuts and woodcuts put her squarely in the American Scene or Regionalist art movement of the 1930s. She exhibited widely: the 1939 New York World's Fair, the Philadelphia (Pennsylvania) Print Club, the Southern States Art League (award-winner), the Birmingham (Alabama) Museum of Art, the High Museum of Art in Atlanta, Georgia, the Florida Federation of Art, the Brooklyn (New York) Museum and the National Academy of Design in New York City.

She was also known for her handicrafts, especially jewelry and tiles.

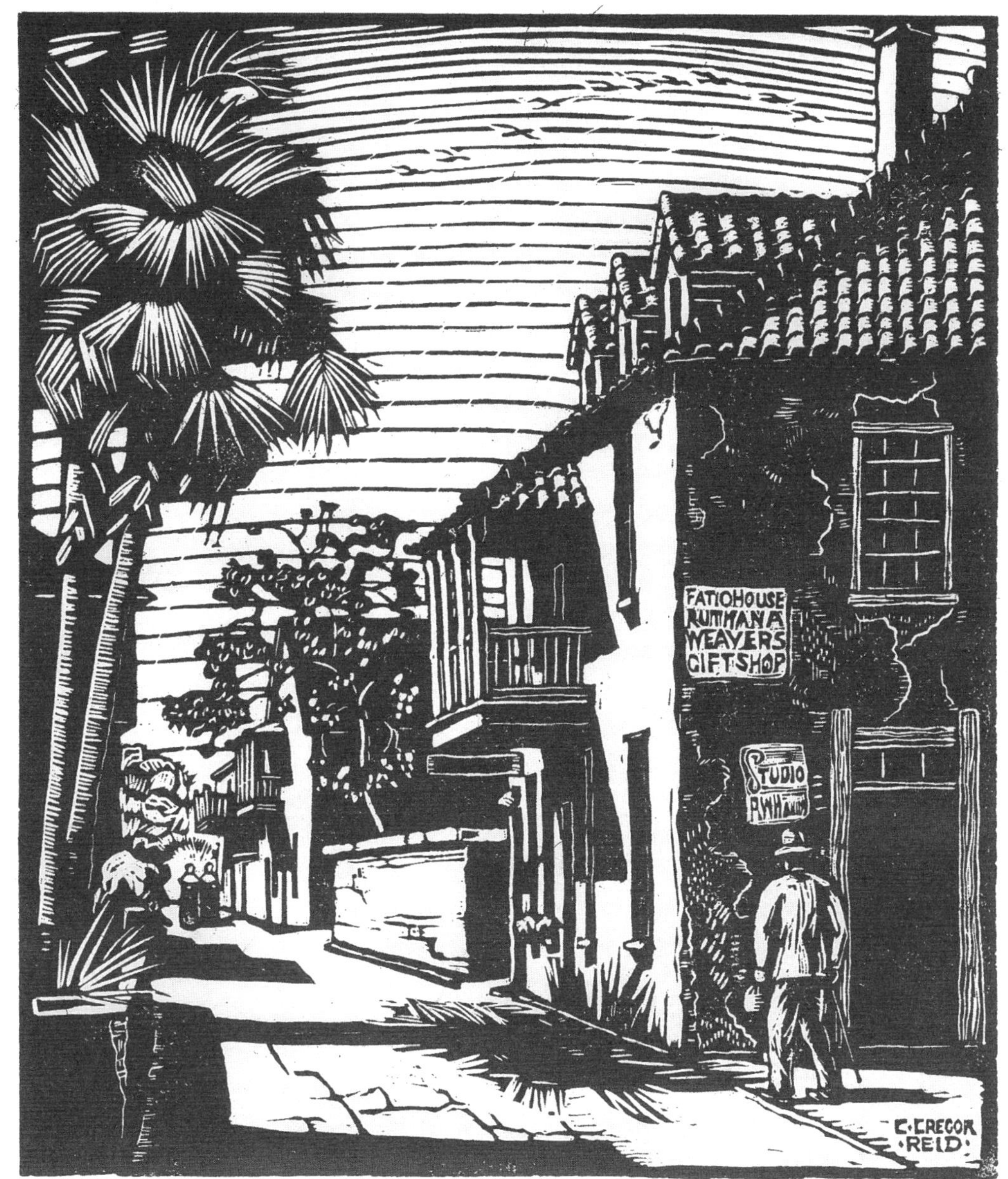
FATIOHOUSE
RUTHMANA
WEAVERS
GIFTSHOP
STUDIO
C. GREGOR
REID

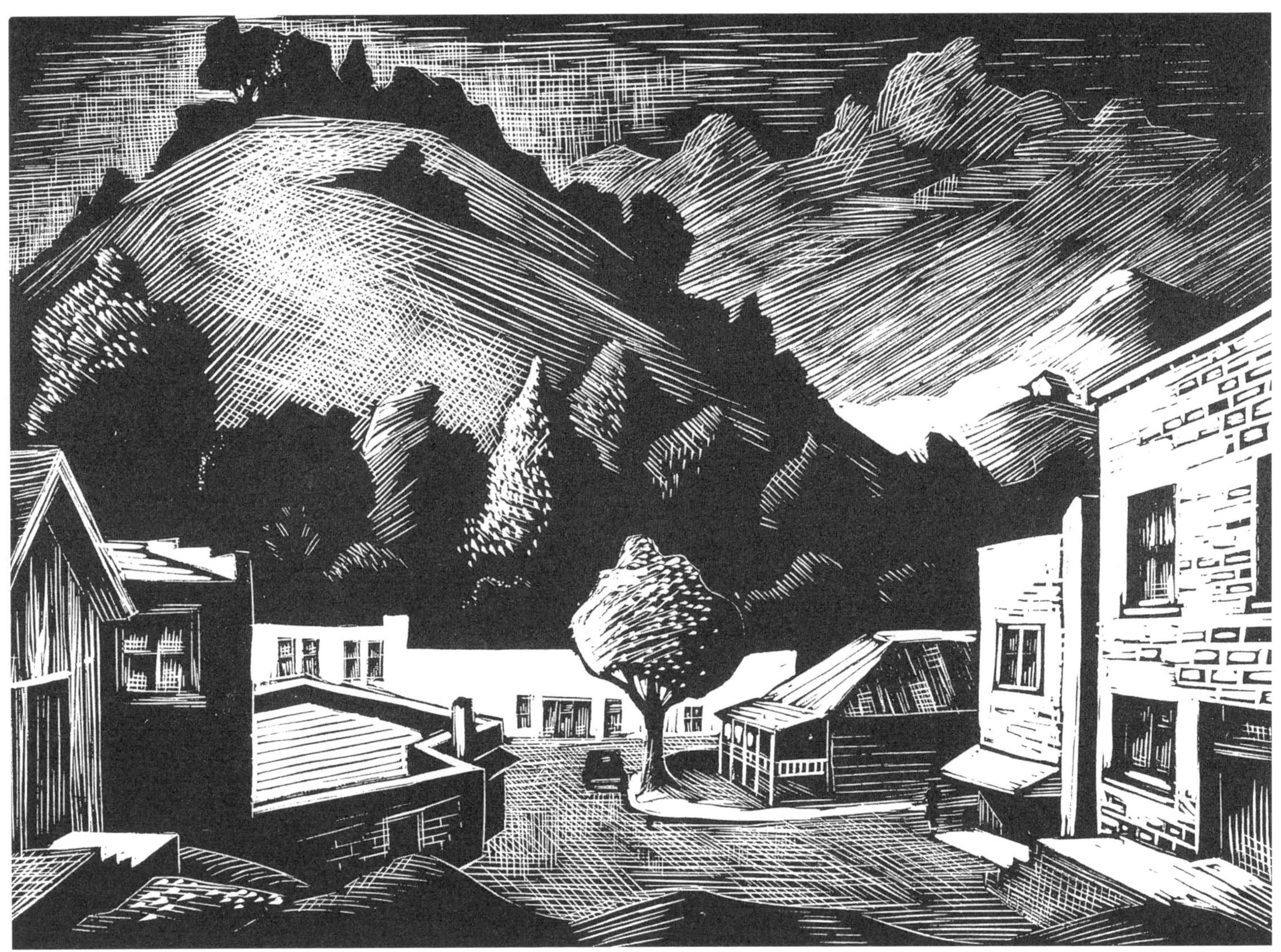

Malcolm Arnett

MALCOLM ARNETT (1905-1992) described himself as a man who "combined farming with printmaking and the painting of murals and other landscape oils."

Manchester, Kentucky
block print
4 1/2 x 6 3/8 inches

He was born in Cairo, Illinois, but sometimes said he was born in Kentucky. His family moved across the Ohio River to the Henderson, Kentucky, area in 1906. The family dairy farm was at Dixie, in Henderson County, and Arnett was graduated from the Dixie High School in 1929.

During the 1930s and early 1940s he studied at Western Kentucky University in Bowling Green with legendary artist-teacher Ivan Wilson and at the Kansas City Art Institute in Kansas City, Missouri, with American Regionalists Thomas Hart Benton and John de Martelly. Arnett worked at the William Rockhill Nelson Gallery of Art (Nelson-Atkins Museum of Art) during his years in Kansas City.

Upon his return to Henderson County, he began seriously exhibiting. He had a print show at Western in 1950 and appeared in the *Tri-State Art Exhibitions* at the Evansville (Indiana) Museum of Arts, History and Science during much of the 1950s. In 1986 he shared wall space with outsider artist Henry Faulkner and others in the exhibition *Paintings and Drawings by Kentucky Artists from the Collection of Greene A. Settle Jr.* at Transylvania University in Lexington. There was an important show in 1989 at the Capital Gallery of Contemporary Art in Frankfort, and the same gallery put on a retrospective in 1993.

Arnett was known for his hand-printed Christmas cards which inspired a 1982 book, *Landmarks: Forty Prints from Forty Years of Printmaking*. Arnett, whose self-description comes from the book, wrote that his prints "developed from careful pencil drawings made on location. A few are illustrations of actual places, but usually I have made radical changes to conform to an idea; at other times, the sketches are only a point of departure."

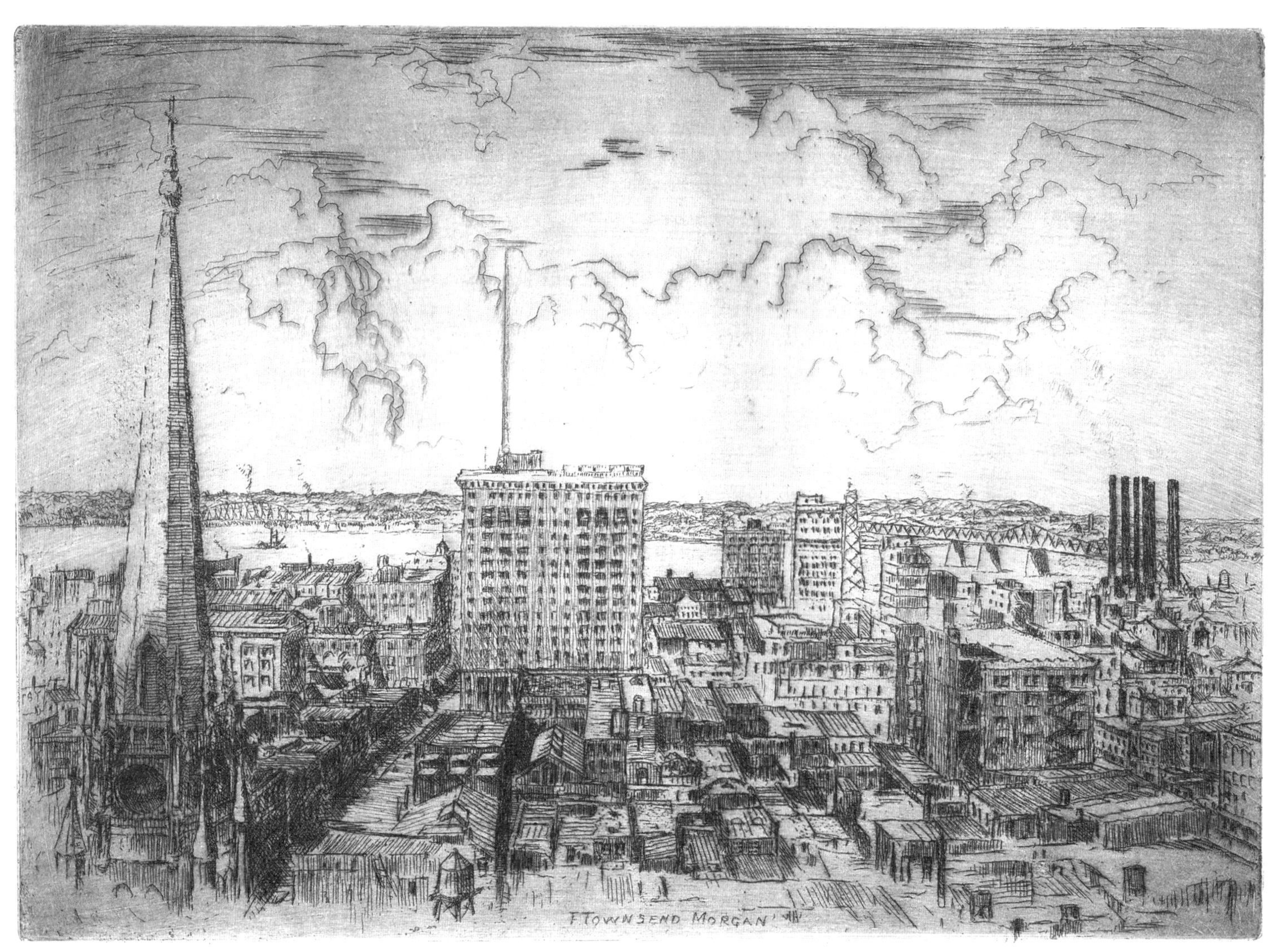
F. TOWNSEND MORGAN

F. Townsend Morgan

Hard times turned **FRANKLIN TOWNSEND MORGAN**'s artistic hobby into a living.

Morgan (1883-1965) was a native of New York City, where he received his training at the Pratt Institute and the Art Students League. He was making prints as early as 1912, but he was earning his living in the family steel business. The company went bankrupt in the Great Depression, and Morgan turned to his art.

He got a job in Philadelphia, Pennsylvania, with the federal Public Works of Art Project. He fit in with the local art scene and was associated with the Print Club, the Sketch Club and the Pennsylvania Academy of the Fine Arts. He also picked up some etching tips from renowned American etcher Joseph Pennell. Other federal arts jobs became available, and Morgan worked in the Virgin Islands and Key West, Florida.

Morgan exhibited frequently and widely in the 1930s, winning awards such as the Society of American Etchers' J. Frederick Talcott Prize in 1935. He liked to capture views of cities and picturesque locations. The Talcott prize, for example, was for a view of Key West. Morgan depicted other cities in Florida and locations in Maryland.

According to a label attached to the Louisville print, the Newth Morris Box Corp. of Baltimore, Maryland, "engaged" Morgan "from year to year … to create his impression of American cities on copper plates." Judging from a history of the company, the Louisville plate dates from the early 1940s.

It was during that same period that Morgan took the job of artist-in-residence at St. John's College in Annapolis, Maryland. He maintained his Key West ties and died in Florida.

Morgan's work is in the collections of the New York Public Library, the Library of Congress and the U.S. Treasury Department, Washington, D.C., and art museums in Pennsylvania and New Jersey.

A retrospective, *Avocation to Vocation: Prints by F. Townsend Morgan*, was held at the University of Georgia in 2017.

Louisville
etching and aquatint
edition number 74
7 x 9 3/4 inches

The *Courier-Journal* obituary for **CHARLES WINSTON HABERER** (1905-1958) described him as "a Louisville artist who pioneered in souvenir etchings of historic and scenic spots," completely ignoring his work in fine printmaking.

Haberer was a 1922 graduate of Male High School and trained at the Louisville Art School with printmaker A. J. Van Leshout and portraitist Sudduth Goff. He studied at the American Academy of Art in Chicago, Illinois, and the School of the Art Institute of Chicago. Returning home, he worked as a commercial artist at the *Louisville Herald-Post* newspaper and Bacon's department store.

In 1941 Haberer was the subject of a *Newsweek* magazine article about his success selling mass-produced notecards and Christmas cards, all illustrated with an original etching. The cards, with their historic and sentimental scenes, were sold in gift and souvenir shops. World War II interrupted, and Haberer served in the European Theater with the U.S. Army Air Corps. He continued his commercial work and his etching upon his return to Louisville. Many of Haberer's prints, both in etching and lithography, date from the 1930s and 1940s.

He was a member of the Prairie Print Makers, the Chicago Society of Etchers and the Southern States Art League and exhibited with the Philadelphia (Pennsylvania) Society of Etchers, the Rocky Mountain Printmakers and the Washington (D.C.) Water Color Club. His prints are in the collections of the Library of Congress and the Smithsonian American Art Museum in Washington; the University of Massachusetts Amherst; the Kentucky Historical Society; the Denver (Colo.) Art Museum; the University of Louisville; the New York Public Library; the Art Institute of Chicago; the Spencer Museum of Art, Lawrence, Kansas; and many more.

A retrospective was mounted in 1967 by the Merida Gallery in Louisville, and the accompanying catalog put Haberer's output of fine-art etchings at about 80 prints.

Palisades, Kentucky River
etching
31/100
4 7/8 x 8 3/4 inches

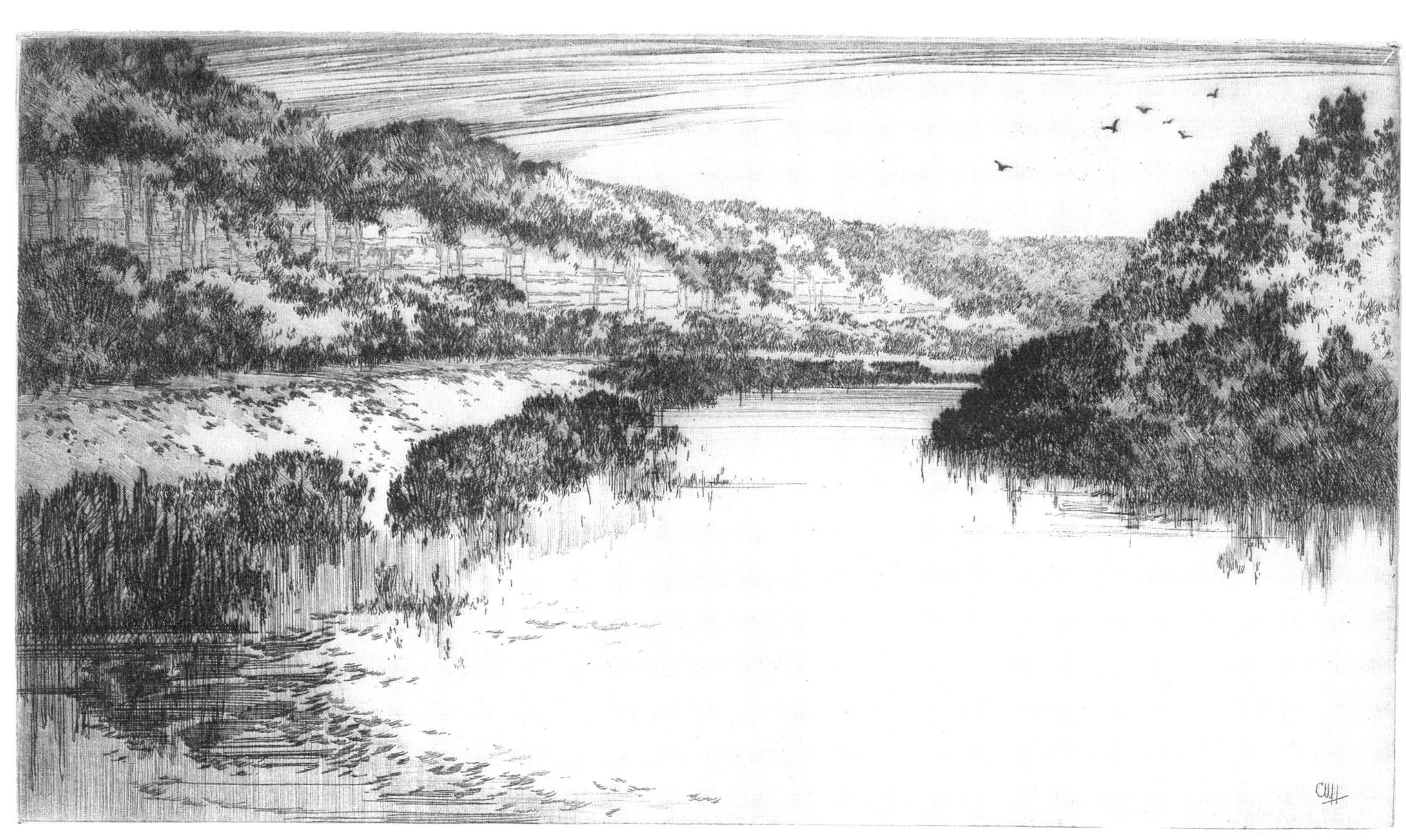

Ralph Fletcher Seymour

RALPH FLETCHER SEYMOUR (1876-1966) was an Illinois native closely involved in the artistic and literary life of Chicago. He was as celebrated for his fine-press books as for his prints.

His etching career spanned several decades, apparently starting in the 1910s. He came into his own in the 1930s, when he could be grouped with those American Scene artists of the time identified with Chicago. He traveled widely looking for picturesque views of life in the United States and was celebrated for his work inspired by the Southwest. He exhibited widely, taking an award in the 1936 Philadelphia (Pennsylvania) Print Club show and appearing in an exhibition at the Louisville (Kentucky) Art Center, also in 1936. He showed in the Hoosier Salon, too. He helped found the Chicago Society of Etchers and taught at the School of the Chicago Art Institute.

His literary career varied from writing about "the greatest paintings" in the Louisville *Courier-Journal* and being the first publisher of Harriet Monroe's groundbreaking *Poetry* magazine. The limited-edition books he printed were distinguished by his hand-decorating and -lettering. In 1945 he published his illustrated autobiography, *Some Went This Way: A Forty Year Pilgrimage Among Artists, Bookmen and Printers.*

Vevay is a town in southeastern Indiana across the Ohio River from Ghent, Kentucky.

Ferry at Vevay
etching
1940
8 x 10 inches

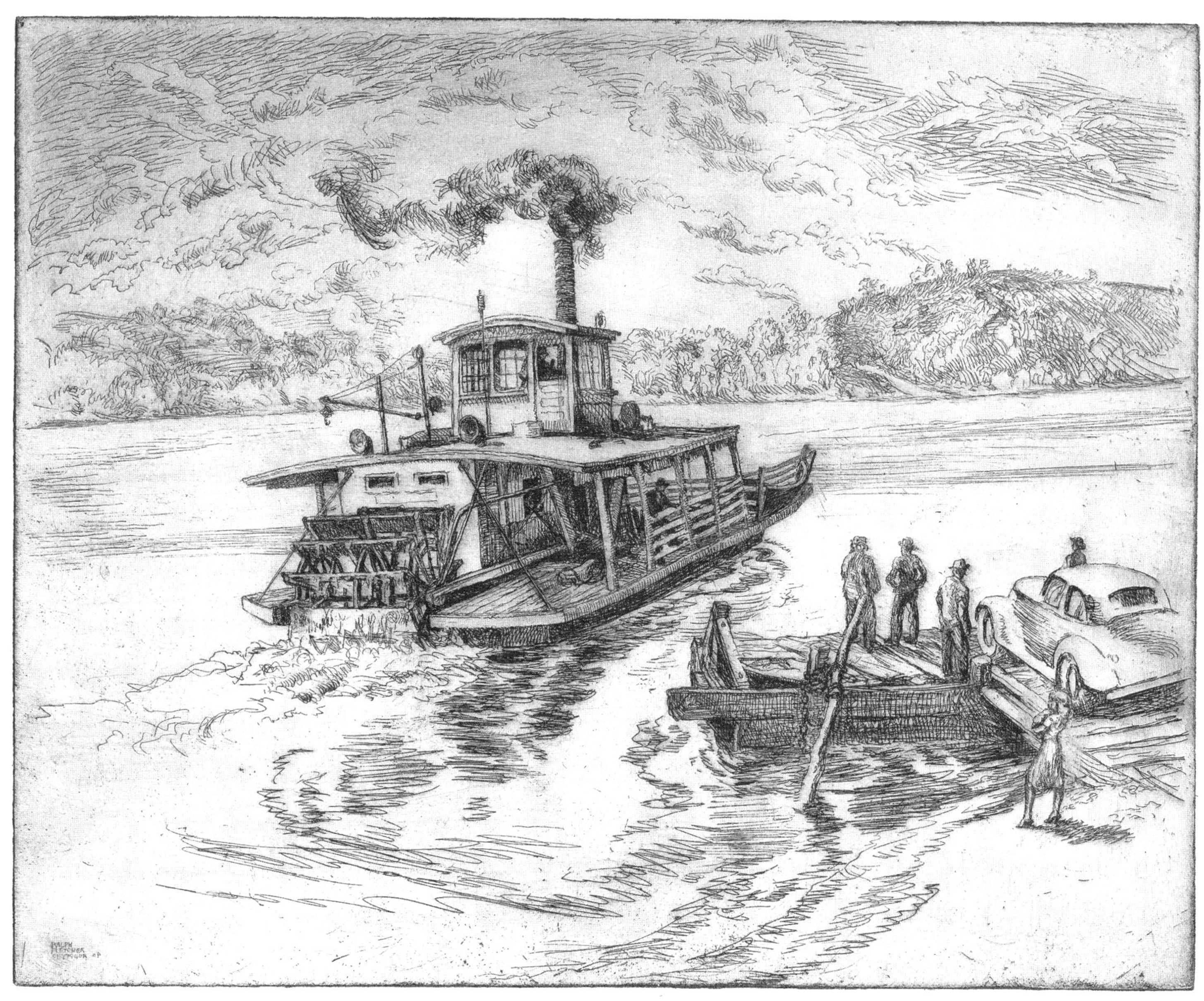
RALPH
FLETCHER

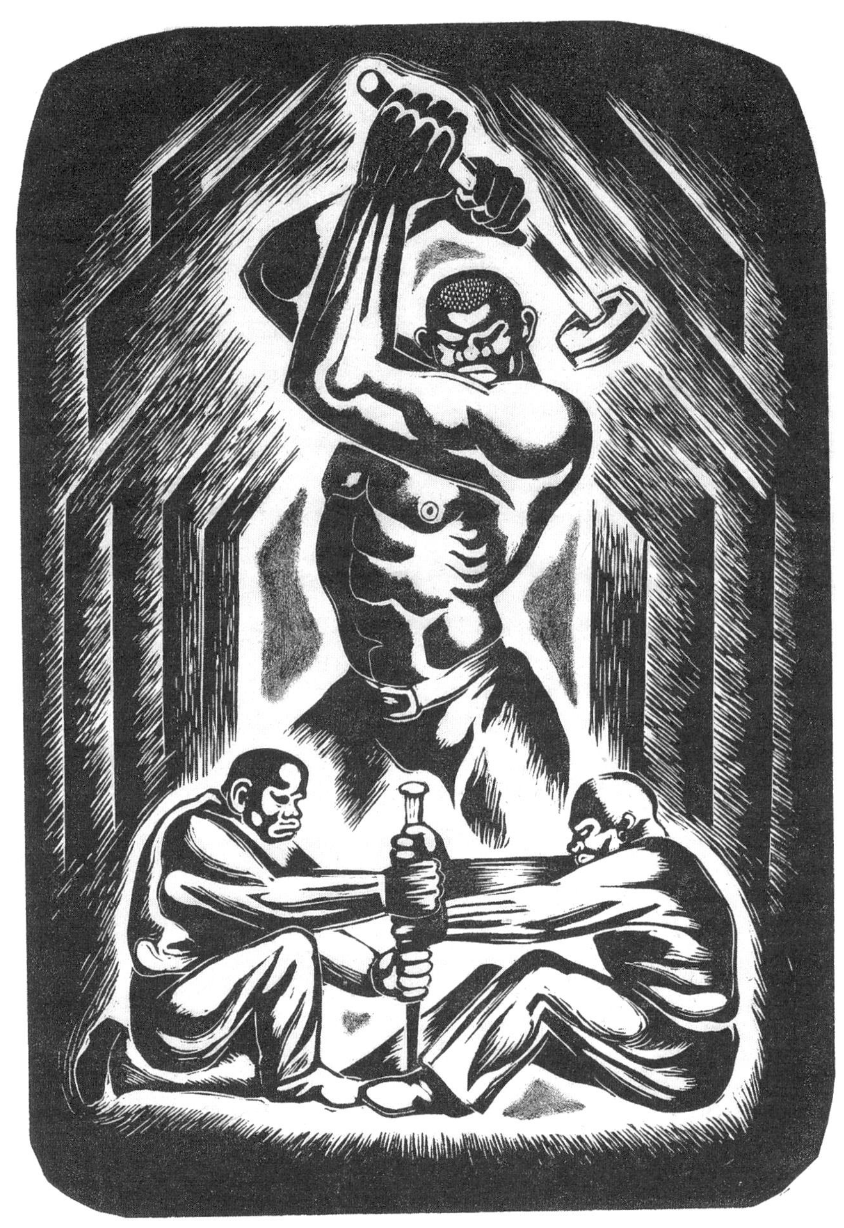

F. Long

FRANK WEATHERS LONG, muralist, easel painter and printmaker, was one of Kentucky's greatest contributors to the American Scene/Social Realism art movement of the 1930s.

Long (1906-1999) was a Tennessee native interested in art from an early age. He studied at the School of the Art Institute of Chicago and the Pennsylvania Academy of the Fine Arts in Philadelphia. He traveled to France and studied at the Academie Julian in Paris. He returned to America during the Depression and established a studio in Chicago. He came to Kentucky to help his father, Clifton J. Long, also a painter, finish a project at a Lexington movie house and settled in Berea.

He executed federally funded murals in Kentucky – Louisville, Morehead and Berea – and in Illinois, Indiana, Maryland and Oklahoma. "Long painted as many murals for 1930s post offices as any other single artist," Sue Bridwell Beckham wrote in the 1991 catalog for an exhibition at the University of Kentucky, *Of Mountains and Music: Frank W. Long.* The university boasts Long murals, done for the Margaret I. King Library.

Long was one of four Kentuckians whose work was selected to represent the art of the South in *American Art Today,* the 1939 World's Fair exhibition of contemporary painting in New York City. Art critic Sadakichi Hartmann deemed Long one of America's 10 most influential artists showing at the fair. That same year Long's paintings filled a wall at the Speed Art Museum in Louisville, "lending a modern note," the *Courier-Journal* reported, to a *Recent Acquisitions and Loans* exhibition.

Long served in the Army during World War II, returning to Berea and taking up the making of jewelry. He studied lapidary art in New Mexico, where he was involved in the federal Indian Arts and Crafts program, and moved there in the late 1960s.

Long was not a prolific printmaker. He worked in wood engraving and almost exclusively in the 1930s. His "John Henry" was done as a prize for the 1941 annual high school exhibition at the University of Kentucky.

John Henry
block print
edition number 1
1941
10 x 7 inches

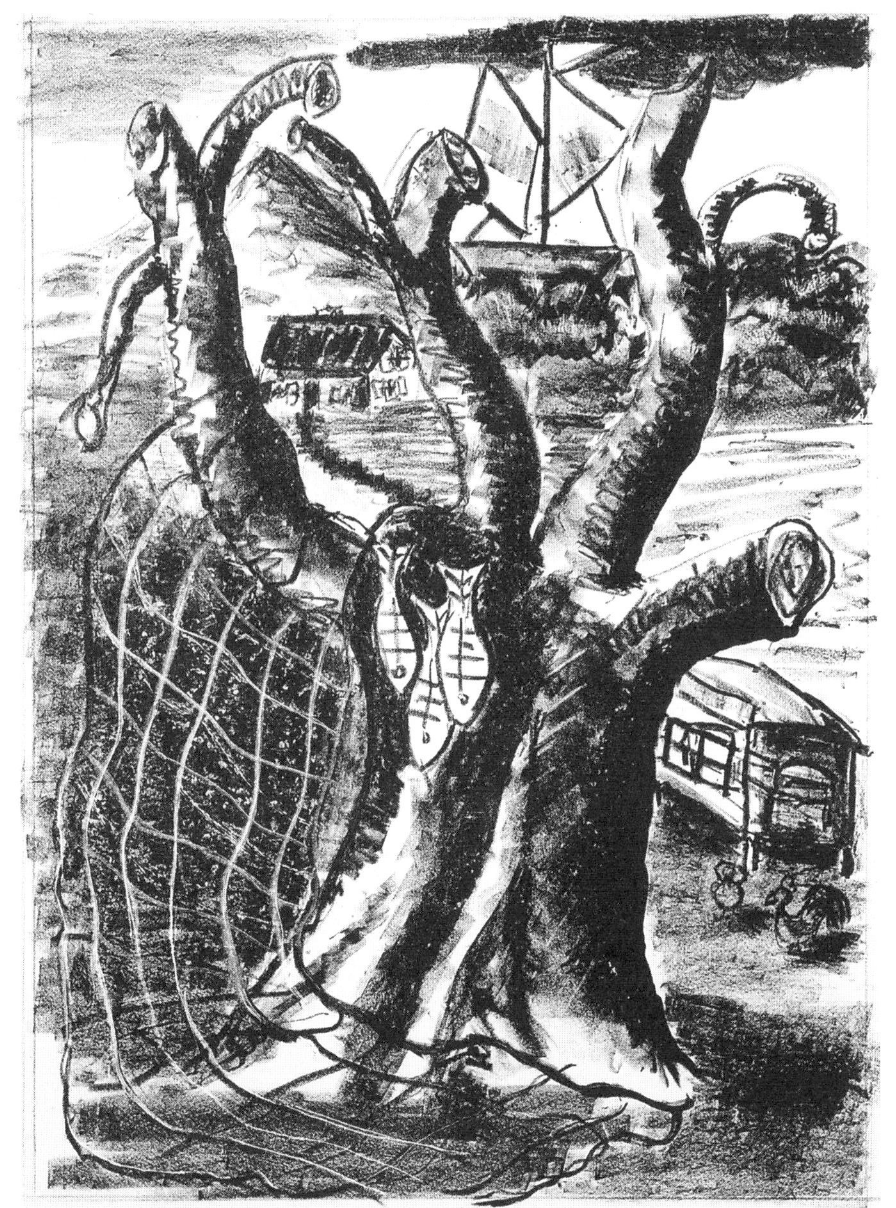

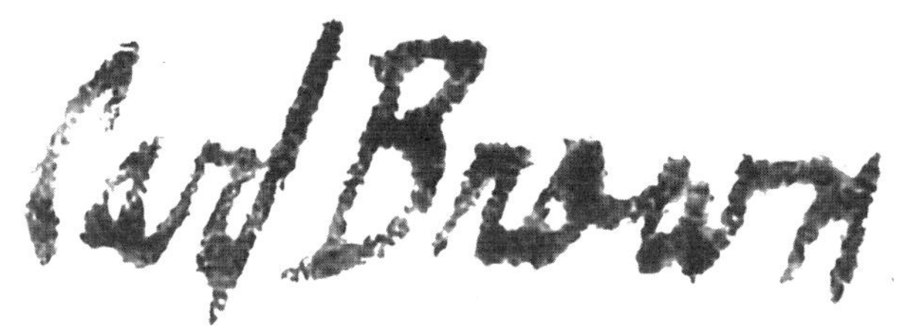

CARL BROWN (1917-2016) was a Louisville, Kentucky, native who began his studies at the Louisville Art Center in 1940. World War II interrupted his training, and he served in the Army in the Pacific Theater. Returning to Louisville, he worked as a store window decorator and continued his instruction at the Art Center with Fayette Barnum, who was the director, Mary Spencer Nay, Constance Clark Willis and Romuald Kraus. He later studied there with Worden Day and came face to face with Cubism.

Miss Barnum had a long relationship with the artist colony at Provincetown, Massachusetts, sending many of her students there for further work. She did the same with Brown, introducing him to Peter Hunt, known as an "American furniture folk artist," and Brown worked in the Hunt studio decorating furniture with European peasant motifs.

In 1954 Brown returned to Louisville after four years of travel that took him to Paris, where he studied with Andre Lhote, and to many Mediterranean countries as well as North Africa. He showed 80 watercolors at Mary Alice Hadley's Little Gallery on Story Avenue, a popular show by newspaper accounts. Brown also had a painting in the Aetna Collection, works acquired through purchase prizes at the Art Center's annual exhibition of Kentucky and Southern Indiana artists. In 1955 Brown had a one-man show at the Weyhe Gallery on Lexington Avenue in New York City. According to an *Art News* notice, Brown showed paintings on wood, wood gathered on Moroccan beaches.

In the 1960s Brown divided his time between Palm Beach, Florida, and Long Island, New York. Long Island was an important art colony, and Brown had a more than nodding acquaintance with such artists as Jackson Pollack and Willem de Kooning. Brown showed at the Ashawagh and Guild halls in East Hampton. He eventually settled in West Palm Beach, Florida, and in 2013 the community honored him with an exhibition, *Carl Brown: Travels After the War.* A catalog by curator Elizabeth Dowdle was published.

Brown also exhibited at the Worth Avenue Gallery and The Society of the Four Arts in Palm Beach.

title unknown
lithograph
1941
13 7/8 x 10 1/8 inches

FRANCIS A. (FRITZ) BADE (1893-1967) talked of himself as more of a salesman that an artist. He was often referred to as a "hobbyist" in the *Courier-Journal* newspaper. Yet he pursued his interest in painting, drawing and etching.

Bade (pronounced bay-dee) was a native of Goshen, Indiana, and an engineering graduate of the University of Michigan. He moved to Louisville and, starting in 1928, was the president of the Bade-Cummins Manufacturing Co., which made automotive parts, until it was sold in 1950. He was a manufacturers' representative for steel companies at the time of his death.

In the 1940s the president of the Liberty National Bank & Trust Co., Merle E. Robertson, had the idea of giving original works of art to depositors as Christmas presents. Robertson himself was known as a photographer, carpenter and etcher, and he decided on etchings as gifts. He commissioned Bade to do some of those popular prints. Bade was an associate member of the Society of American Etchers and had an etching in its 1942 annual exhibition in New York City.

Robertson was also aware of Bade's other "hobby," creating wood-inlay mosaic murals. In 1950 he hired Bade to design and install four wood panels in the Liberty branch at Fifth Street and Broadway. The panels – each one six feet long and four feet high – showed a river scene with a steamboat, a coal mine, a sorghum mill and a tobacco auction.

Bade's inlay murals could also be found in Louisville homeowners' bars.

Live Oak
etching
1944
5 x 6 7/8 inches

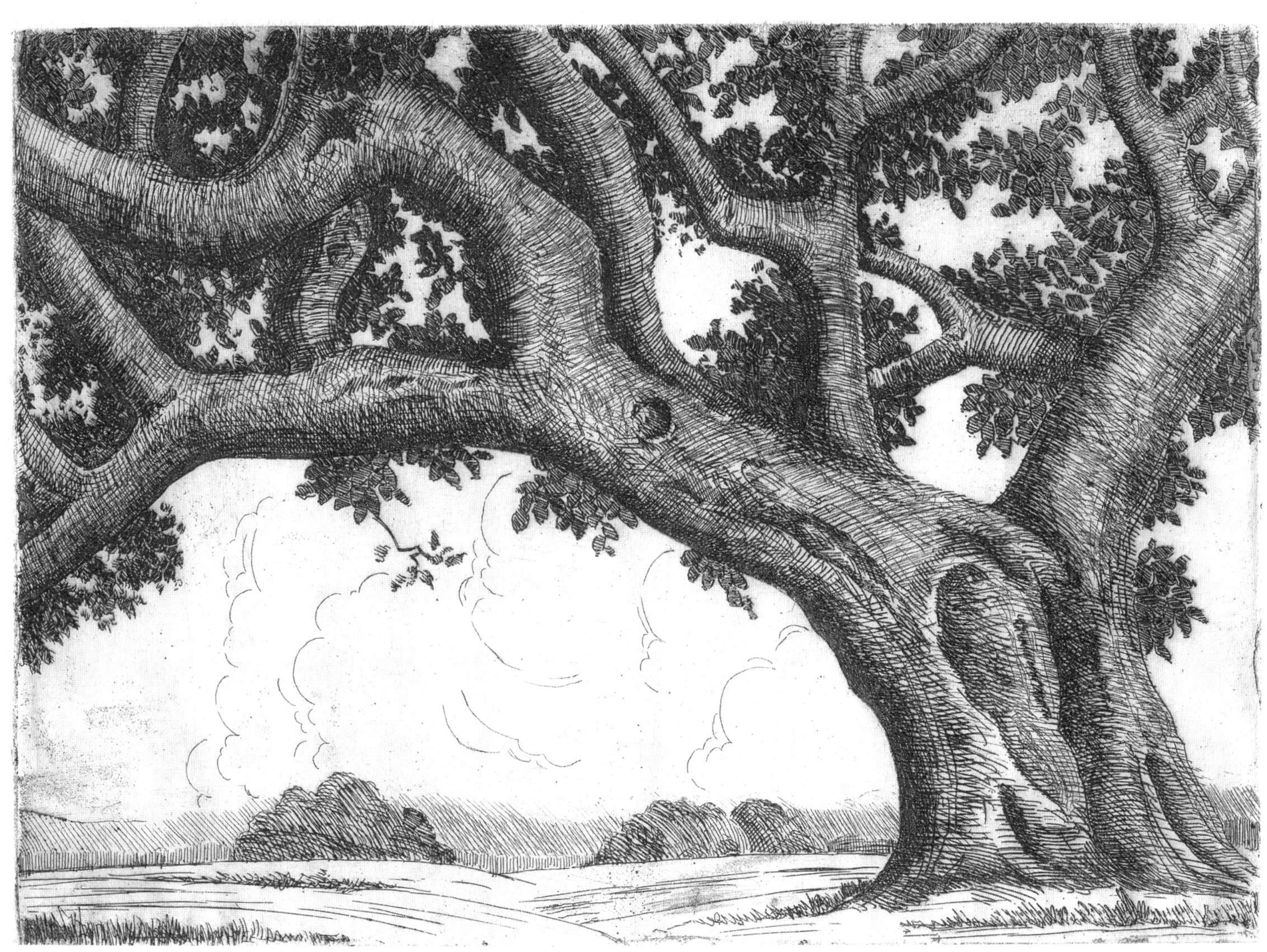

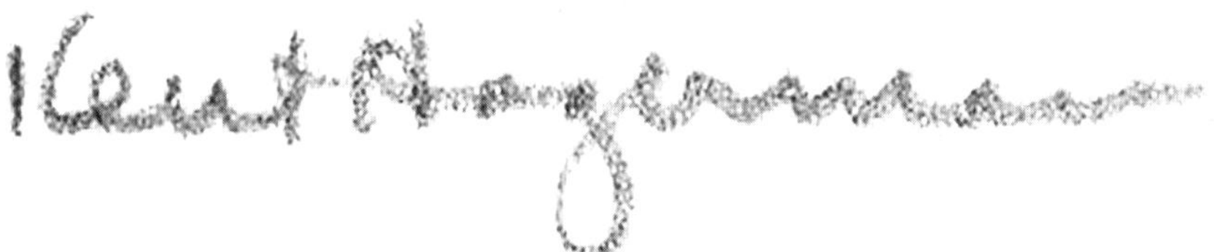

Starting in 1946, **KENT HAGERMAN** was responsible for at least 15 etchings distributed annually by the Liberty National Bank & Trust Co. of Louisville, Kentucky. Hagerman depicted scenes varying from the city's old Haymarket to the Kentucky Derby.

Each etching came with information about the scene and the artist. Hagerman, Merle E. Robertson, bank president, would point out, "journeyed to Kentucky to make the sketch" for his etching.

Hagerman (1893-1978) had settled in Lakeland, Florida, in 1933. He was an Ohio native and studied at the Cleveland School of Art (Cleveland Institute of Art). He served in France in World War I and used some of that time to further his training at the Sorbonne in Paris. He was involved in an engraving company for some years before moving to Florida.

His etchings of Chicago, Illinois, scenes done in the 1940s and 1950s are heavily collected, as are his Florida scenes.

He was an honorary member of the Kappa Pi International Art Honor Society, founded in 1911 at the University of Kentucky in Lexington, and was represented in its collections, both permanent and touring. He has etchings in the Smithsonian American Art Museum in Washington, D.C., the Art Institute of Chicago and the Polk Museum of Art at Florida Southern College in Lakeland.

He is also known as Will K. Hagerman, William Kent Hagerman and William Kay Hagerman.

Kentucky Tobacco Patch
etching
1946
6 1/2 x 9 3/8 inches

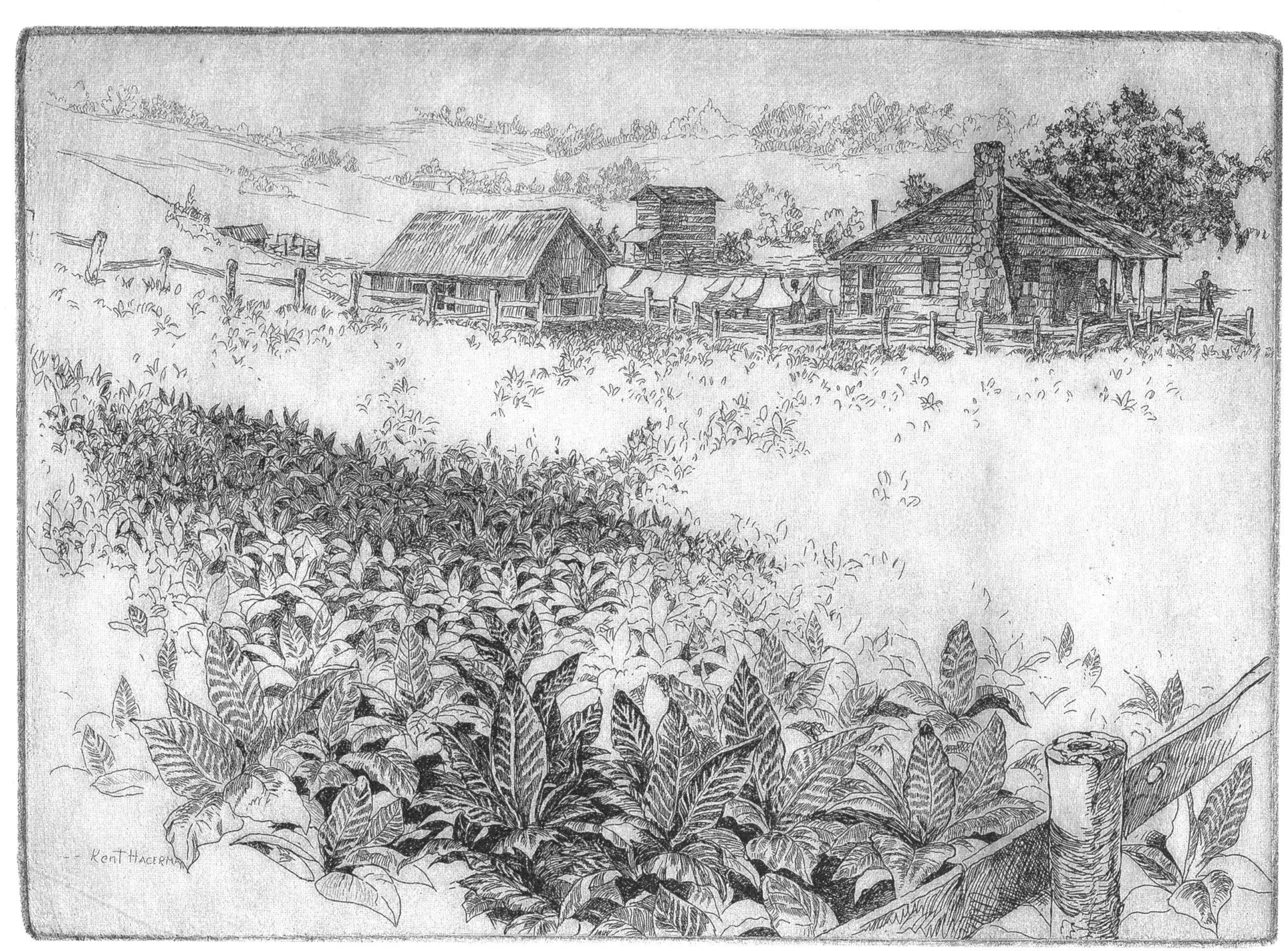
Kent HAGERMA

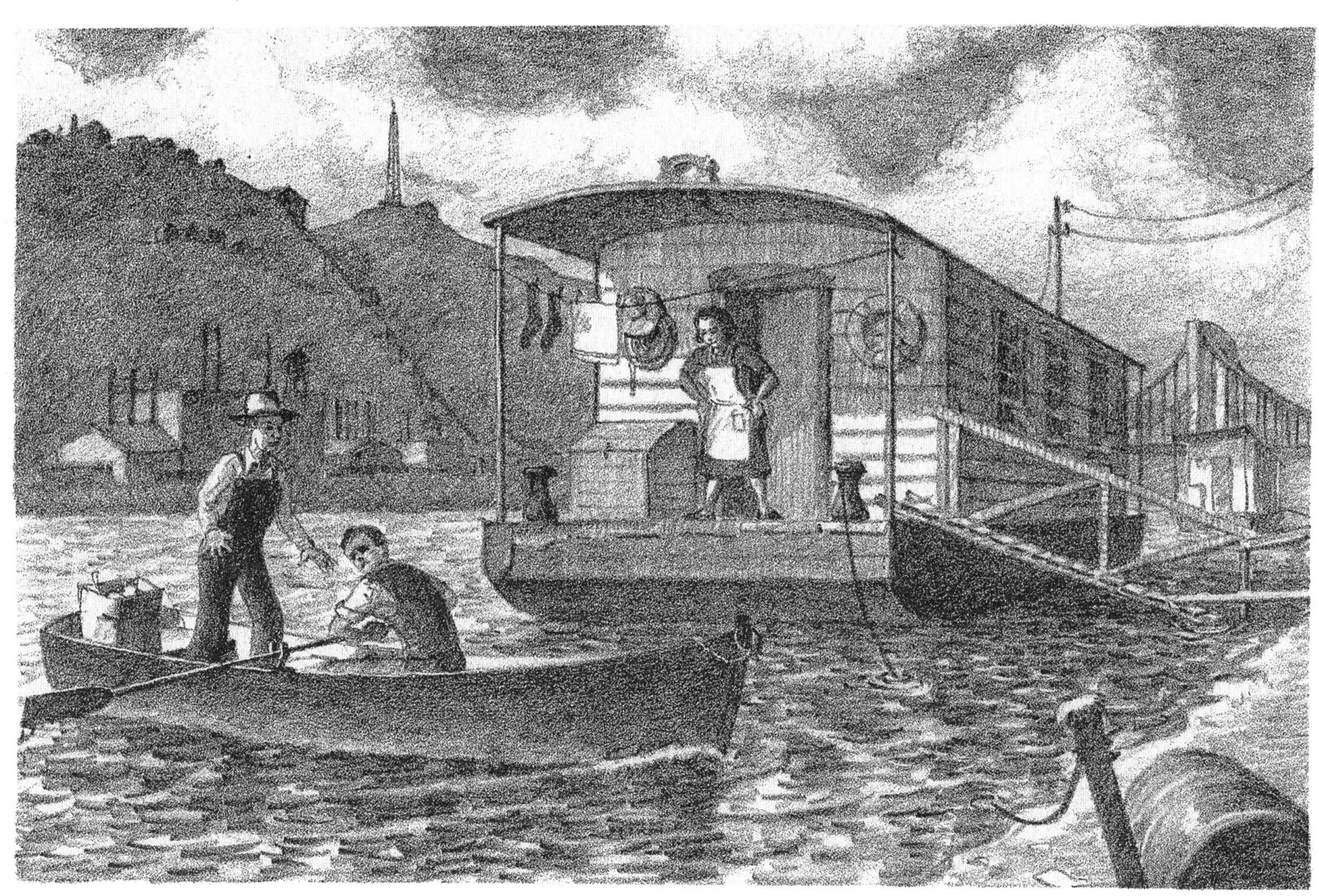

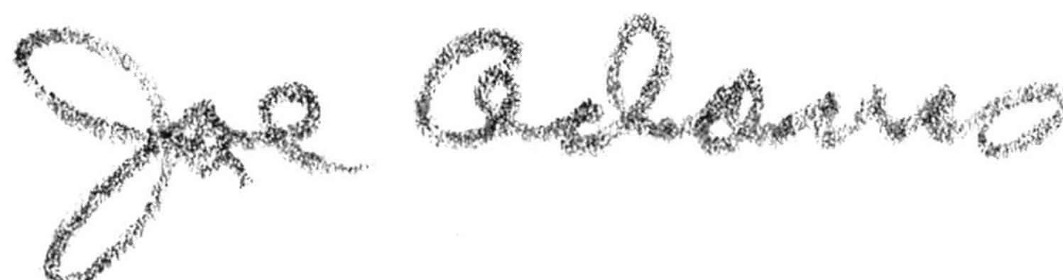

JOE ADAMS was a lithographer of Cincinnati, Ohio, scenes. Unfortunately, there is virtually no information about him to be found. Two of his lithographs, including the shanty-boat one opposite, turned up in a bookstore in New Orleans, Louisiana, in 2015. Adams was working in the 1940s, and his style bears some resemblance to that of Cincinnati artist Kenneth W. Ozier.

This 1946 shanty-boat view is from the Kentucky bank of the Ohio River with Cincinnati's Mount Adams in the distance. Regional and national artists captured that particular way of life from the 1920s through the 1940s.

title unknown
lithograph
1946
5 1/4 x 8 1/4

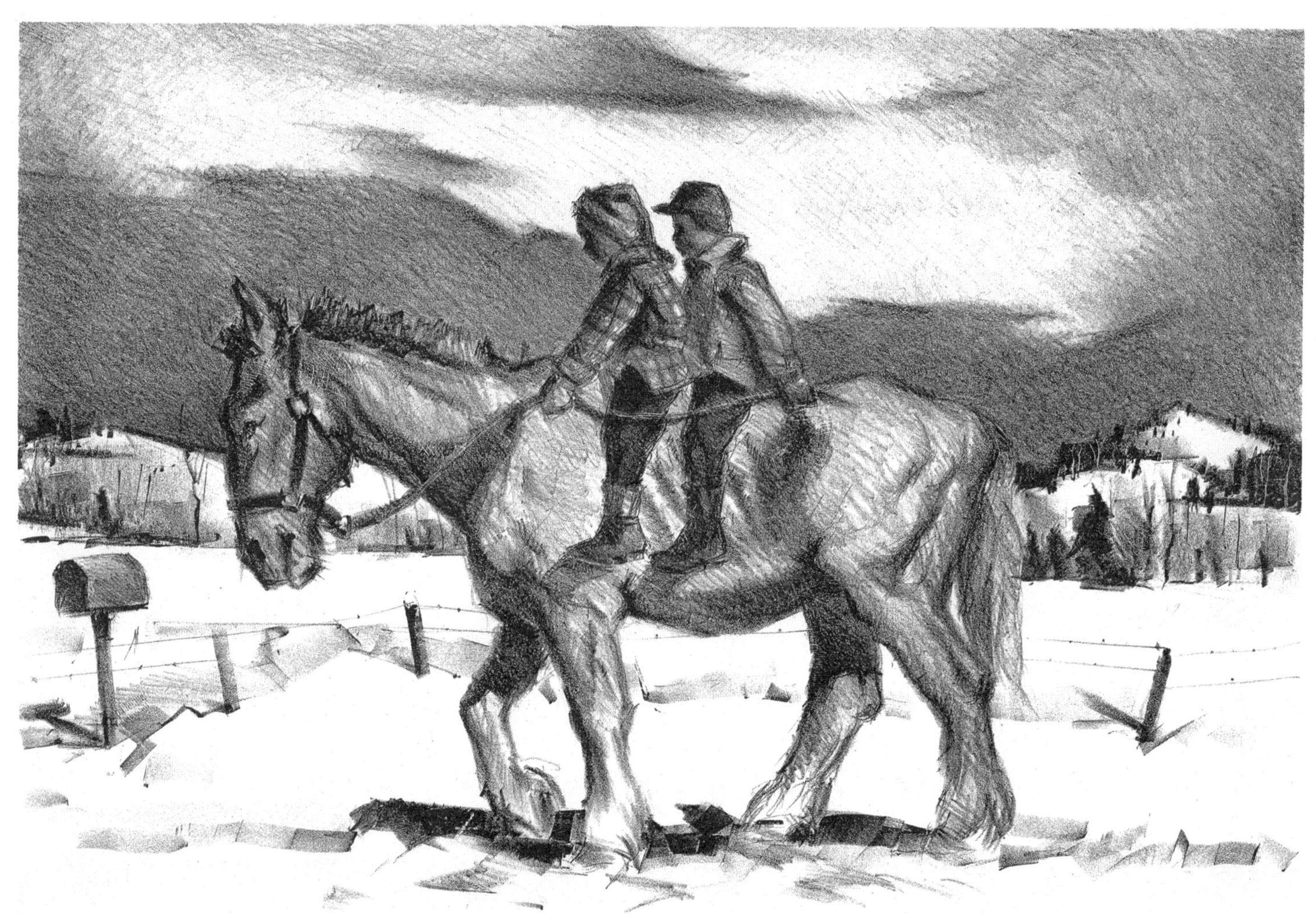

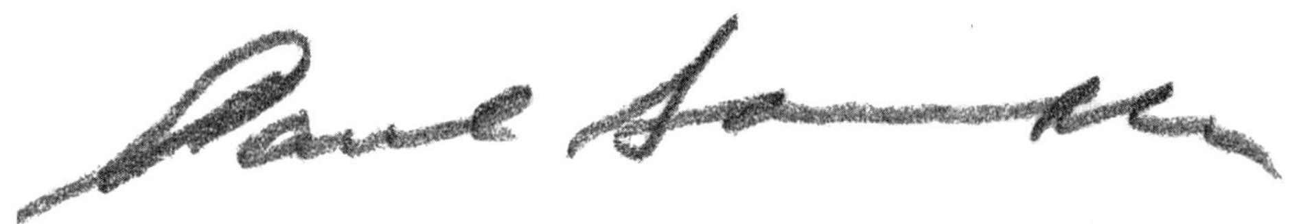

PAUL STARRETT SAMPLE (1896-1974) was a native of Louisville, Kentucky, but, as he told the *Courier-Journal Magazine* in 1951, his father was a civil engineer and "we traveled a great deal never living in one place very long."

Sample entered Dartmouth College in New Hampshire in 1916, graduating from the school in 1921 after serving in World War I. He taught art for a decade at the University of Southern California. He was offered a position as artist-in-residence by Dartmouth, and he accepted after a European sojourn. Sample's wife, Sylvia , was from Vermont, and the family settled there. Sample described himself in the *Courier-Journal* article as an "ardent trout and salmon fisherman" who enjoyed playing the flute.

Sample said he "identified with no particular school or group of American Paintings," but his choice of subject matter – rural New England life – and his style mark him firmly as an American Regionalist. In addition to his painting, Sample worked as an illustrator for such companies as General Motors and Maxwell House Coffee and for popular magazines.

The *Courier-Journal* feature reported that "forty-seven museums and important public collections own his work, and he has won 13 of the most important art awards." Among those collections was the Seagram Collection of Contemporary Art by Kentucky Artists.

Sample showed at the Metropolitan Museum of Art's important *American Painting Today – 1950* exhibition, and in 1952 Louisville's Speed Art Museum held a Sample one-man exhibition. The only painting in the Speed show with any reference to the artist's home state was *Blue Grass Pastures* of 1946, which had been acquired by the Chesapeake and Ohio Railway Co.

Rural Delivery
lithograph
1948
9 3/4 x 13 3/4 inches

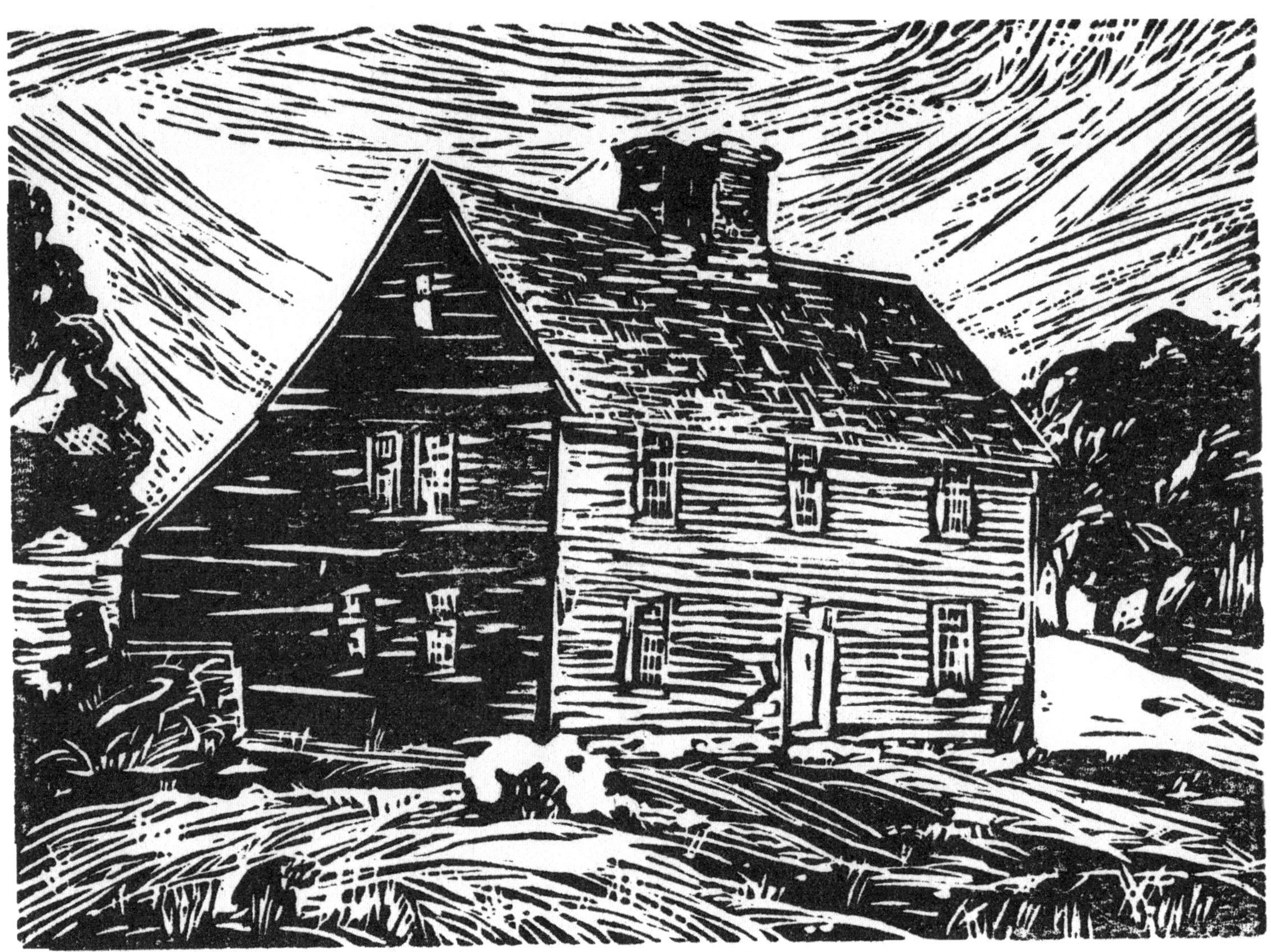

Carolyn Dunbar

CAROLYN SMITH DUNBAR (1894-1968) was a native of New York and educated in Massachusetts. She met and married pharmacist Elias A. Dunbar in Philadelphia, Pennsylvania, in 1918. She had worked as an instructor in occupational therapy at the Philadelphia (Pennsylvania) Hospital. Her husband, a graduate of the University of Kentucky, was from the Jamestown area in Russell County, Kentucky, and that's where the couple settled early in their marriage.

The Dunbars are listed as living in Lexington in the 1930s and 1940s, during which time Mrs. Dunbar made the society news as a chaperone at various sorority and other University of Kentucky events. At some point the family moved to Versailles.

Mrs. Dunbar was active in handicrafts, wining prizes as early as 1919 at the Kentucky State Fair with her basketwork, embroidery and handwoven rugs and table covers. As late as 1962 she had an award-winning painting in a Kentucky Federation of Women's Clubs contest. Her interest in printmaking apparently developed while living in Versailles.

Acadian House - 1670
block print
5 x 7 inches

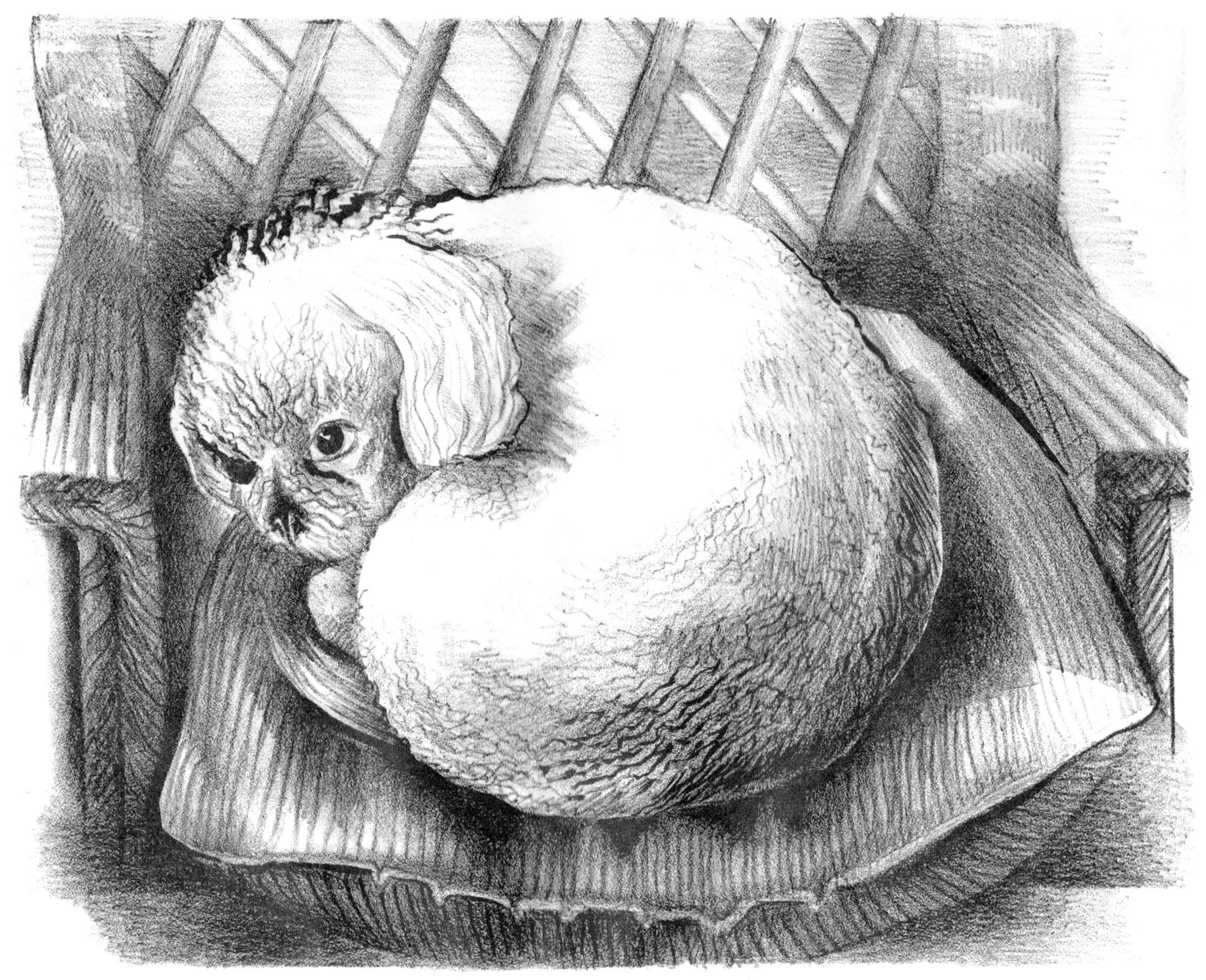

Mary Spencer Nay

Does one describe **MARY SPENCER NAY** (1913-1993) as an artistic polymath or a Renaissance woman? She was a leading figure in Louisville art circles for decades, winning an impressive array of prizes and awards.

Her "espousal and practice of abstract art was a central influence in Louisville … no less because she was a teacher of artists who would themselves be art teachers," art historian Madeline Covi wrote in *Louisville Modern: an era in art* (PFA Press). From 1942 to 1979, Nay taught at the University of Louisville, where she held the Marcia S. Hite Chair of Painting. She also taught at the Art Center Association School, serving as director from 1944 to 1949.

Her style varied, and her work from the 1940s is squarely in the American Scene vein. She was one of four Kentuckians whose works were selected to represent the art of the South in *American Art Today,* the 1939 World's Fair exhibition of contemporary painting in New York City. She also showed in the Metropolitan Museum of Art's *Artists for Victory: An Exhibition of Contemporary American Art* in 1942. In the decades that followed she produced significant abstract work, her printmaking influenced by that of American surrealist Boris Margo and Worden Day, whose style also moved from American Scene to total abstraction.

Nay was a Crestwood, Kentucky, native, and earned her bachelor's and master's degrees from the University of Louisville. She also studied in New York, Cincinnati, Ohio, the art colony in Provincetown, Massachusetts, and Mexico. She married fellow artist and photographer Lou Block in 1951.

She had a retrospective at the Speed Art Museum in Louisville in 1976.

title unknown
lithograph
1940
8 3/4 x 11 inches

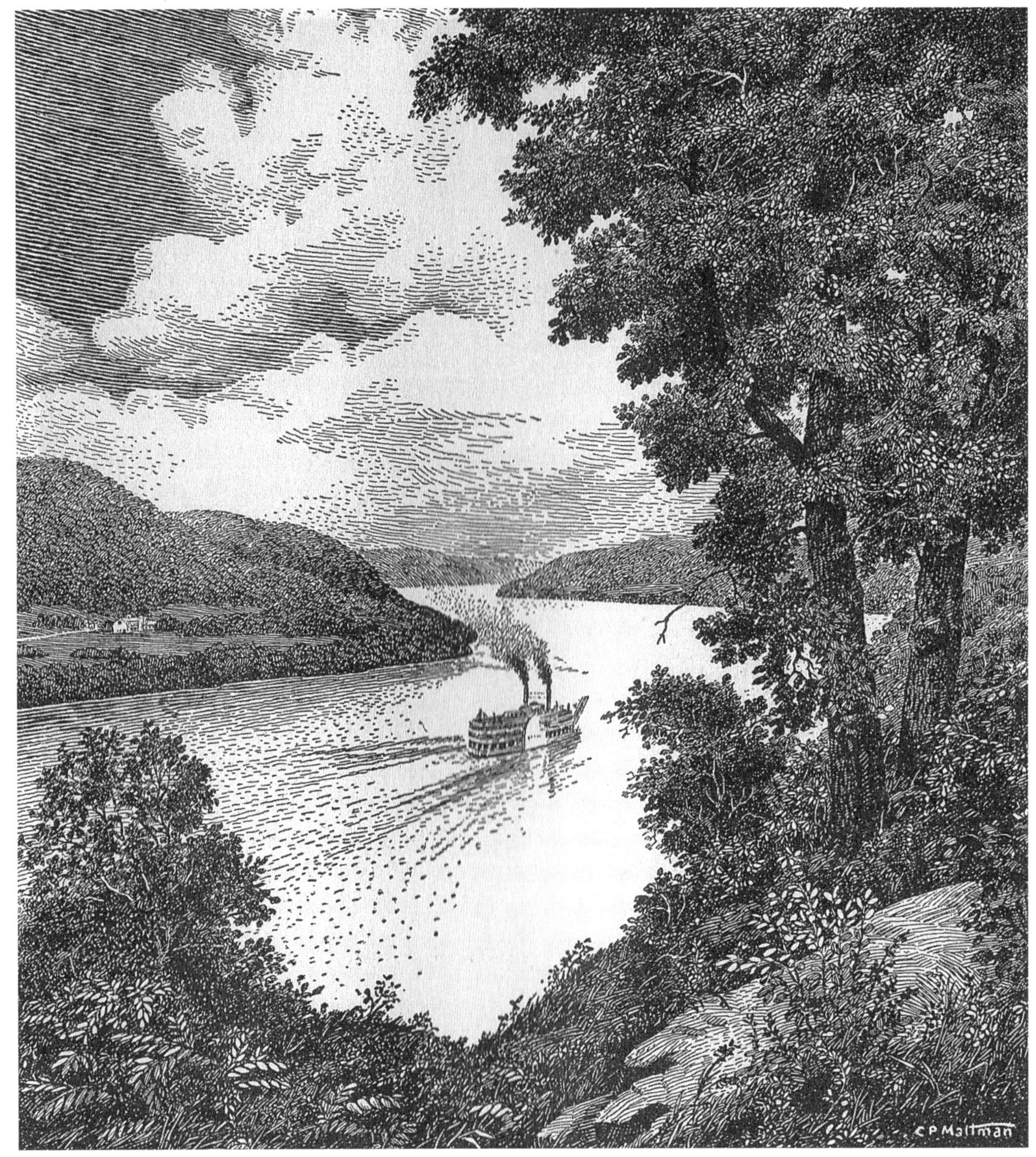
C P Maltman

C P Maltman

CHAUNCEY PUREL MALTMAN (1889-1965) was a commercial artist and book illustrator. The Michigan native studied art through the leading correspondence school of its time, the Federal School of Commercial Designing, headquartered in Minneapolis, Minnesota. He wrote an encomium for the school, published in *Popular Mechanics Magazine* in 1920. He also studied at the American Academy of Art in Chicago, Illinois.

Maltman's career brought him to Louisville, Kentucky, in the early 1940s, where he was the art director for the Doe-Anderson Advertising Agency. He also helped judge the 1943 Woman's Club show.

Before coming to Louisville, he had worked in Chicago, Columbus, Ohio, Grand Rapids, Michigan, and Cleveland, Ohio. He returned to Chicago in the 1940s and at some point moved to California, where he was active in local art groups. Toward the end of his working life, he was known for illustrating children's books.

Our print is from the September 1944 calendar put out by the Wood-Mosaic Co., an international flooring company that was headquartered in Louisville. A *Courier-Journal* review of a Louisville Advertising Club exhibition that year singled out Maltman (misspelled Maltoman) for his "wood-cut-style pen work" on the calendar.

Side-Wheeler Plying Eastward on Ohio River, Northern Boundary of Kentucky and Bordering Much of West Virginia. In these two states five of Wood-Mosaic's severn plants are located.
block print
1944
6 1/2 x 6 inches

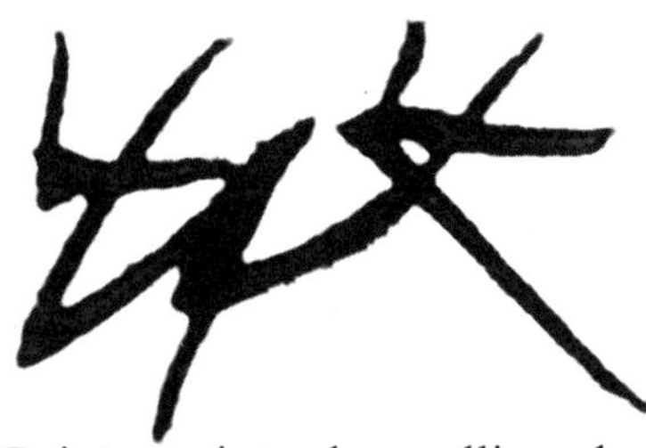

Painter, printmaker, calligrapher, art collector and sometime interior designer, **ULFERT WILKE** came to Louisville, Kentucky, in 1948.

Wilke (1907-1987) was a German native and immigrated to America in 1938. He studied at Harvard University, headed the art department at a Michigan college and joined the U.S. Army in 1942. He was stationed at an Iowa hospital, then worked in Illinois, returning to Iowa to get a master's in art from the State University of Iowa. The Iowa school had a celebrated print program.

Wilke received a joint appointment at the Art Center School and the University of Louisville, where he was an influential teacher of drawing and painting. He traveled widely, having received two Guggenheim fellowships, and on one of his trips he studied Zen calligraphy in Kyoto, Japan. Wilke had a show of 78 works at the University of Kentucky in 1953. He left Louisville in 1962 to live in New York and teach at Rutgers, the State University of New Jersey. He became a colleague and friend of such members of the New York School as Ad Reinhardt, Mark Rothko, Max Beckmann and Robert Motherwell.

Known as an avid art collector, particularly of tribal art, with ties to the international art market, Wilke was hired by the State University of Iowa in 1968 as the founding director of its museum. He retired in 1975 and moved to Hawaii, where he died in 1987.

Wilke had numerous one-man shows and received many awards, including one from the prestigious American Academy of Arts and Letters. His work is held in many museums including the Guggenheim and Whitney museums in New York, the Art Institute of Chicago (Illinois), the San Francisco Museum of Modern Art and the Los Angeles County Museum of Art in California, the National Gallery in Washington, D.C., and the Philadelphia (Pennsylvania) Museum of Art.

He is best known for his large canvas paintings and lithographs inspired by the calligraphic languages of Asia and the Middle East.

Homage a Sengai
lithograph number 7
Fragments from Nowhere:
A Portfolio by Ulfert Wilke
edition 136/200
1958
14 7/8 x 13 7/8 inches

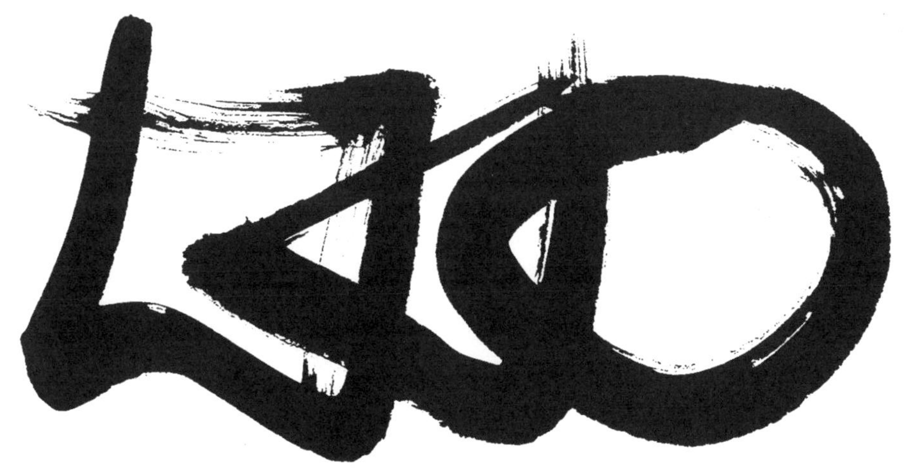

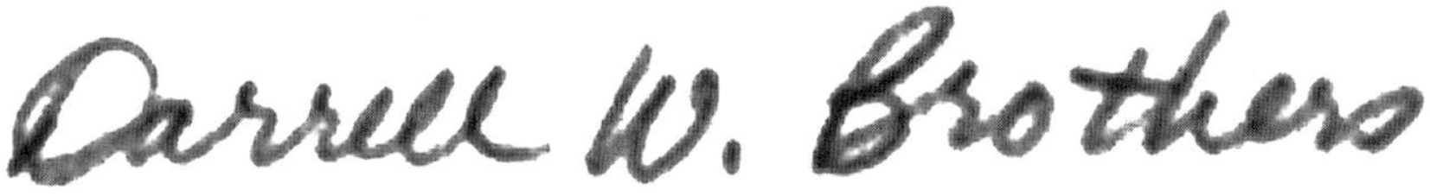

Darrell W. Brothers

DARRELL WILLIAM BROTHERS (1931-1993) was an Alabama native who settled in Covington, Kentucky, after studies in Indiana.

The printmaker, painter and teacher attended the Herron School of Art and Design in Indianapolis and held degrees from Ball State University in Muncie and Indiana University in Bloomington. He served in the U.S. Army during the Korean War.

Starting in the late 1950s, he taught art at the high school level in the Cincinnati Public Schools and evening classes at Northern Kentucky University in Highland Heights. During this time he studied printmaking with the legendary Mauricio Lasansky at the University of Iowa in Iowa City.

In the mid-1960s he moved to Thomas More College in Crestview Hills as an instructor in painting and printmaking. He remained there as head of the art department until his death. Thomas More offers a scholarship in Brothers' name.

Brothers was an abstract artist, then turned to a spare, geometric style and ended up painting the human body. Judging by the number of exhibitions, his most active period appears to have been in the 1970s.

His art is found in the collections of Thomas More, Indiana University and Ball State; the Montgomery (Alabama) Museum of Fine Arts; the Kentucky State Fair and the Speed Art Museum, both in Louisville; Grinnell (Iowa) College; Miami University, Oxford, Ohio; the Chrysler Museum of Art, Norfolk, Virginia; Mount St. Joseph (Ohio) University; and the University of Kentucky in Lexington.

Quarry Landscape #3
etching
edition 10
1958
11 3/4 x 17 1/4 inches

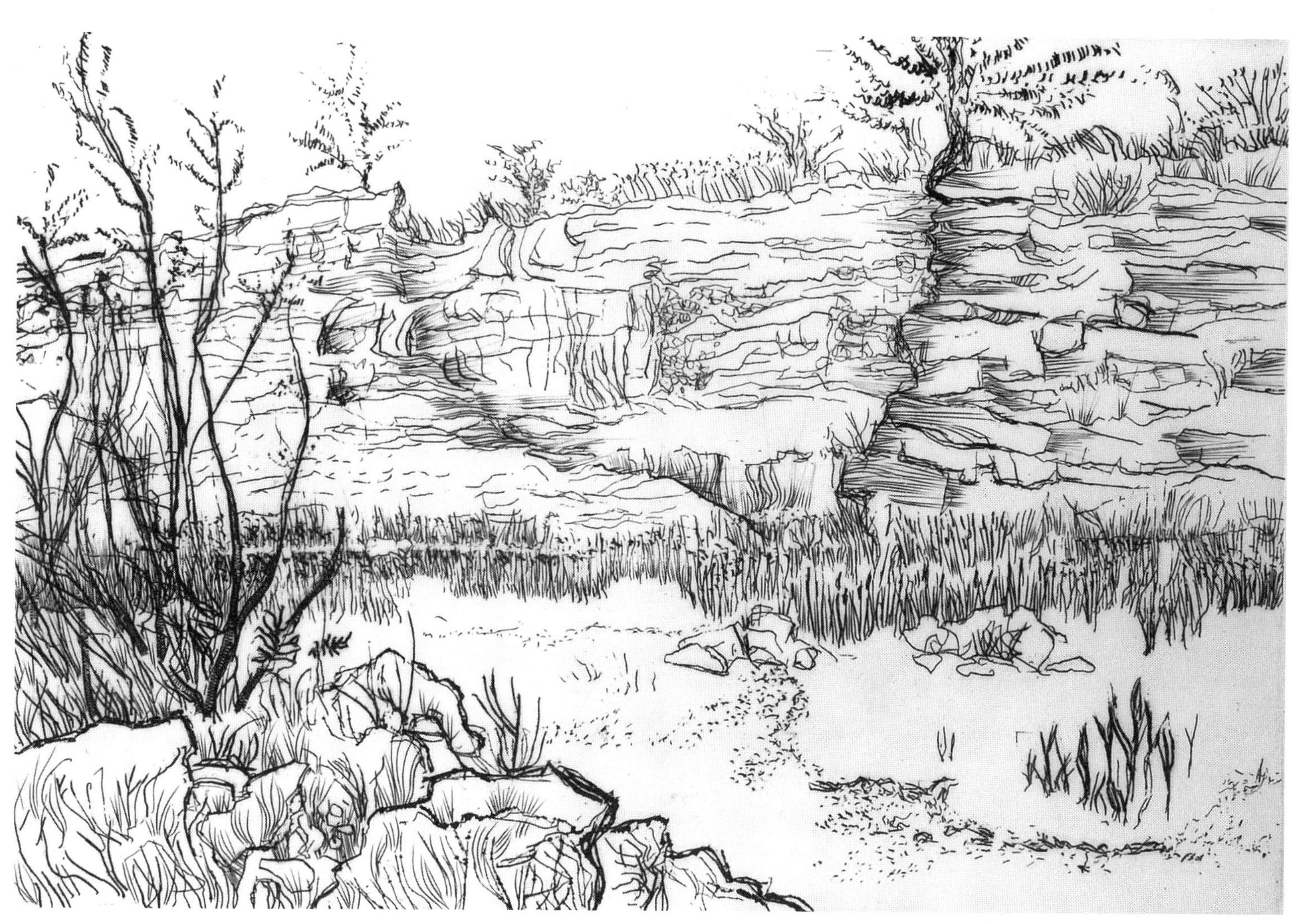

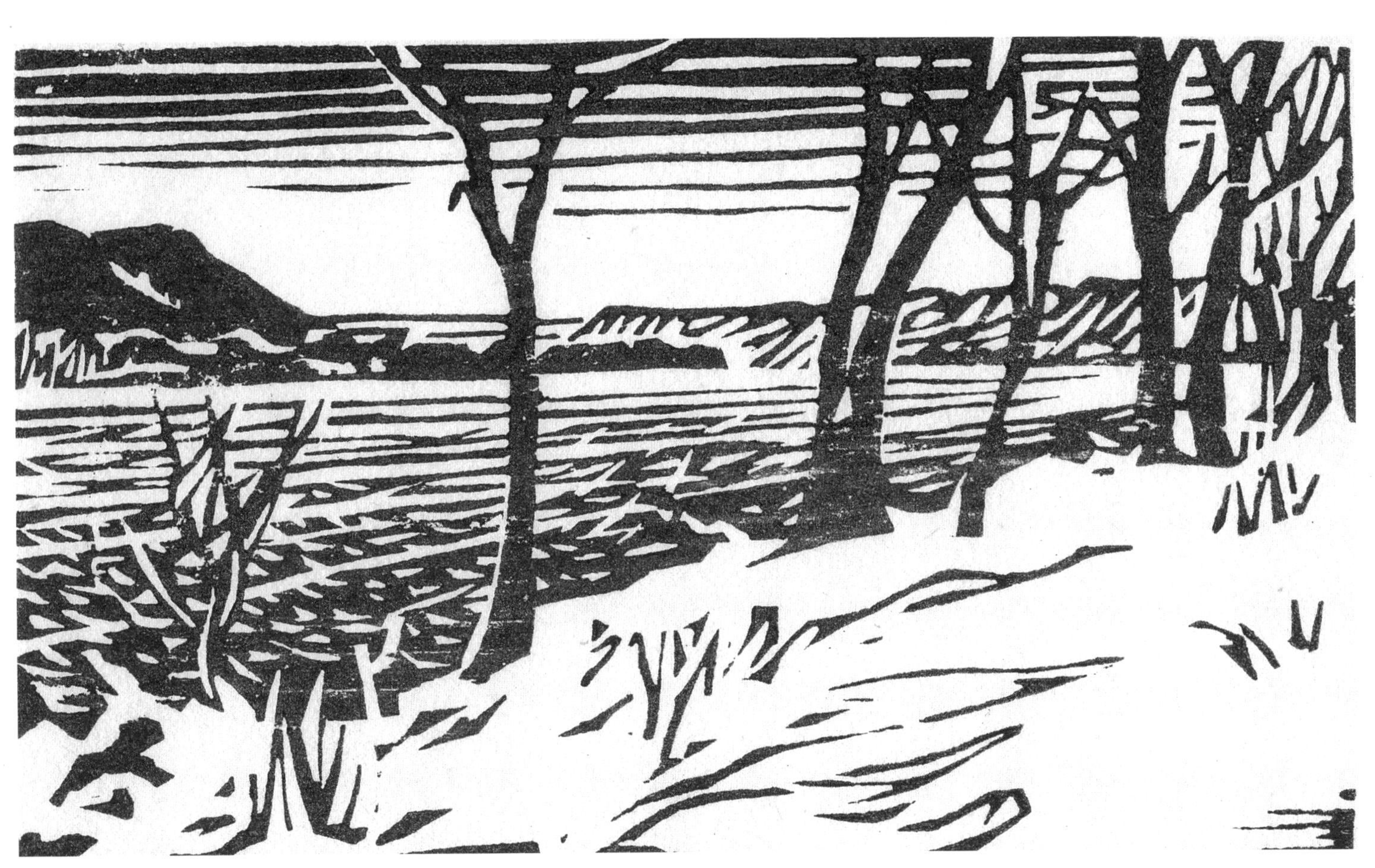

Anna and Harlan Hubbard

HARLAN HUBBARD, artist, author, carpenter, stone mason, architect, boatwright, farmer and fisherman, was born in Bellevue, Kentucky, across the Ohio River from Cincinnati, Ohio. Hubbard (1900-1988) received much of his early training in art in Cincinnati and New York City.

He married Cincinnati librarian Anna Eikenhout (1902-1986) in 1943. The couple traveled down the Ohio and Mississippi rivers in a shanty-boat he built and returned to Kentucky and settled at Payne Hollow, on the Ohio across from Madison, Indiana. They lived in a home they built without any of the conveniences associated with modern life. Hubbard painted and made prints of the world he knew, and Anna, helpmate and fellow musician, added a civilized touch to their Thoreauesque existence.

Plowhandle Point from Payne Hollow
block print
1959
3 1/4 x 5 inches

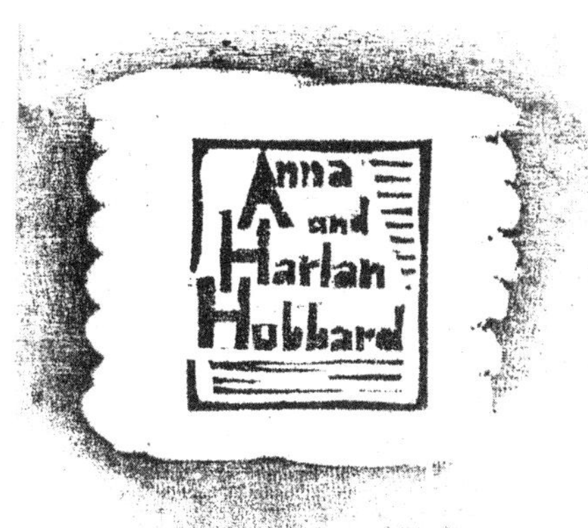

Stamp
block print
2 1/4 x 2 1/8 inches

Hubbard's woodcuts have an American Regionalist look. There are about 180 known examples, most depicting a disappearing river life and landscape. He summed up his career in Wade Hall's 1996 *A Visit with Harland Hubbard* (University Press of Kentucky): "For most of my life I have considered myself an artist, and my artworks are a record of my life's journey."

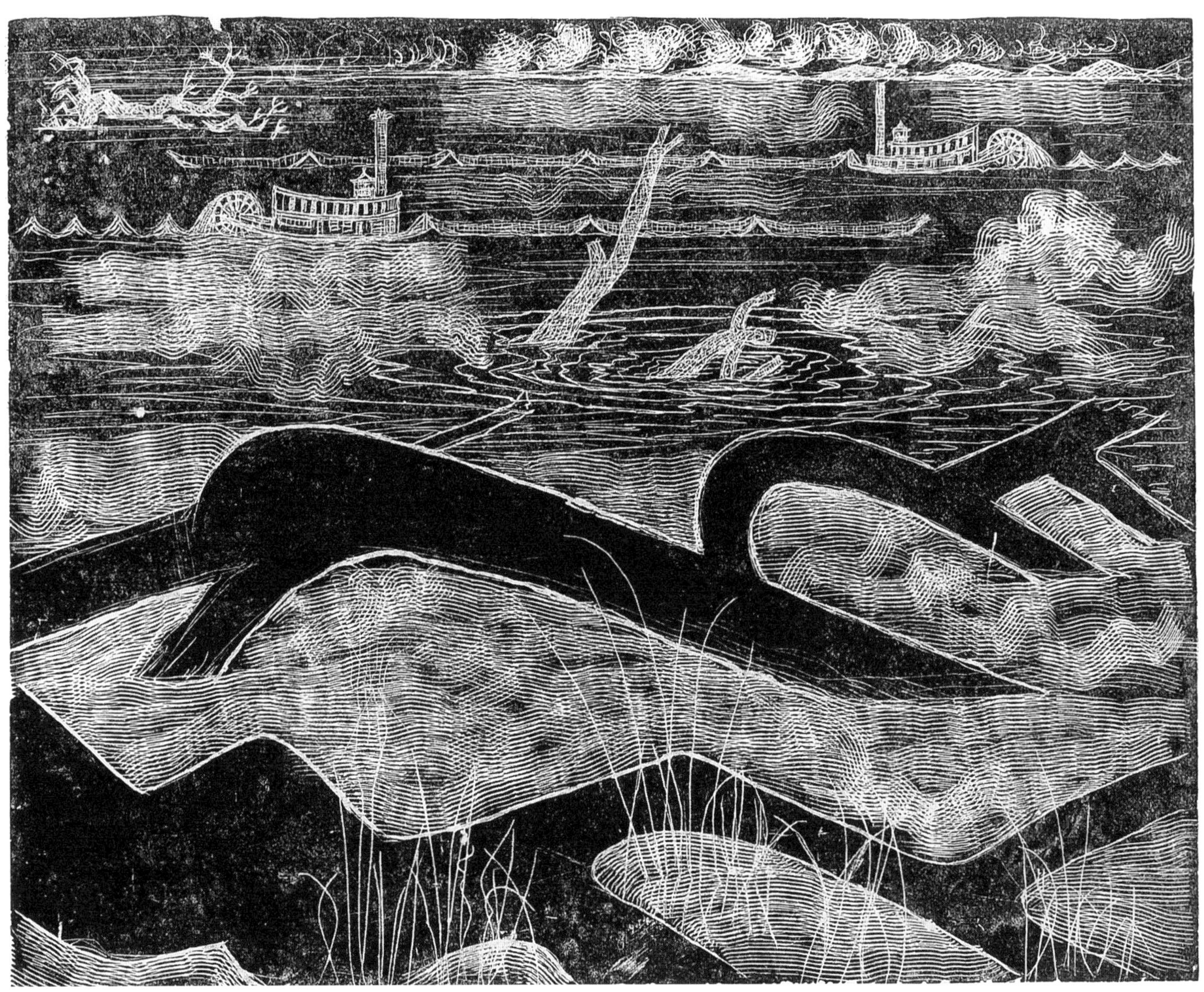

Norman Kohlhepp

NORMAN KOHLHEPP (1892-1986) was an important figure in the Louisville, Kentucky, arts community from the 1930s through his death. His art abounded with river scenes and very colorful horses.

He graduated from duPont Manual Training High School, studied metallurgy at the University of Cincinnati (Ohio), then served in the French Army in World War I. While in Paris, Kohlhepp's first wife and fellow artist, Bostonian Dorothy Smith, prompted his interest in art. Both were influenced by Fauvist painter Andre Lhote. She died in 1964.

"Norman Kohlhepp and the history of art in Louisville are inseparable," *Courier-Journal* art critic Sarah Lansdell once wrote. She praised the engineer-artist as "one of the few who worked to keep the arts alive in the city during the dreary days of the Depression and contributed vitality and talent in later years."

Kohlhepp supported the Louisville School of Art and the Louisville Art Center. His prolific output and generosity as a patron earned him a 1979 retrospective, *50 Years in the Arts,* at the Speed Art Museum. The Smithsonian American Art Museum in Washington, D.C., acquired his *Purple Tree and Ohio River Steamboat* in 1980. Five years later, he was honored by the Kentucky Fair & Exposition Center and the Kentucky Department of the Arts for his support of the state fair art show. Kohlhepp had exhibited at the show steadily from 1936 to 1979. His works are in the collections of the Speed, the Howard Steamboat Museum in Jeffersonville, Indiana, and the University of Louisville. He was the subject of a retrospective, with catalog, at the Howard in 2006.

Kohlhepp produced a large number of prints. He had his pen-and-inks of Louisville scenes reproduced photomechanically in large editions. His fine-art prints were entered in such shows as the *National Print Exhibitions* at the Brooklyn (New York) Museum and the *Regional Exhibitions* at Virginia Intermont College in Bristol, Virginia, where he received the print prize in 1958.

Flood Season
plaster engraving
edition 3/12
1964
18 1/2 x 24 inches

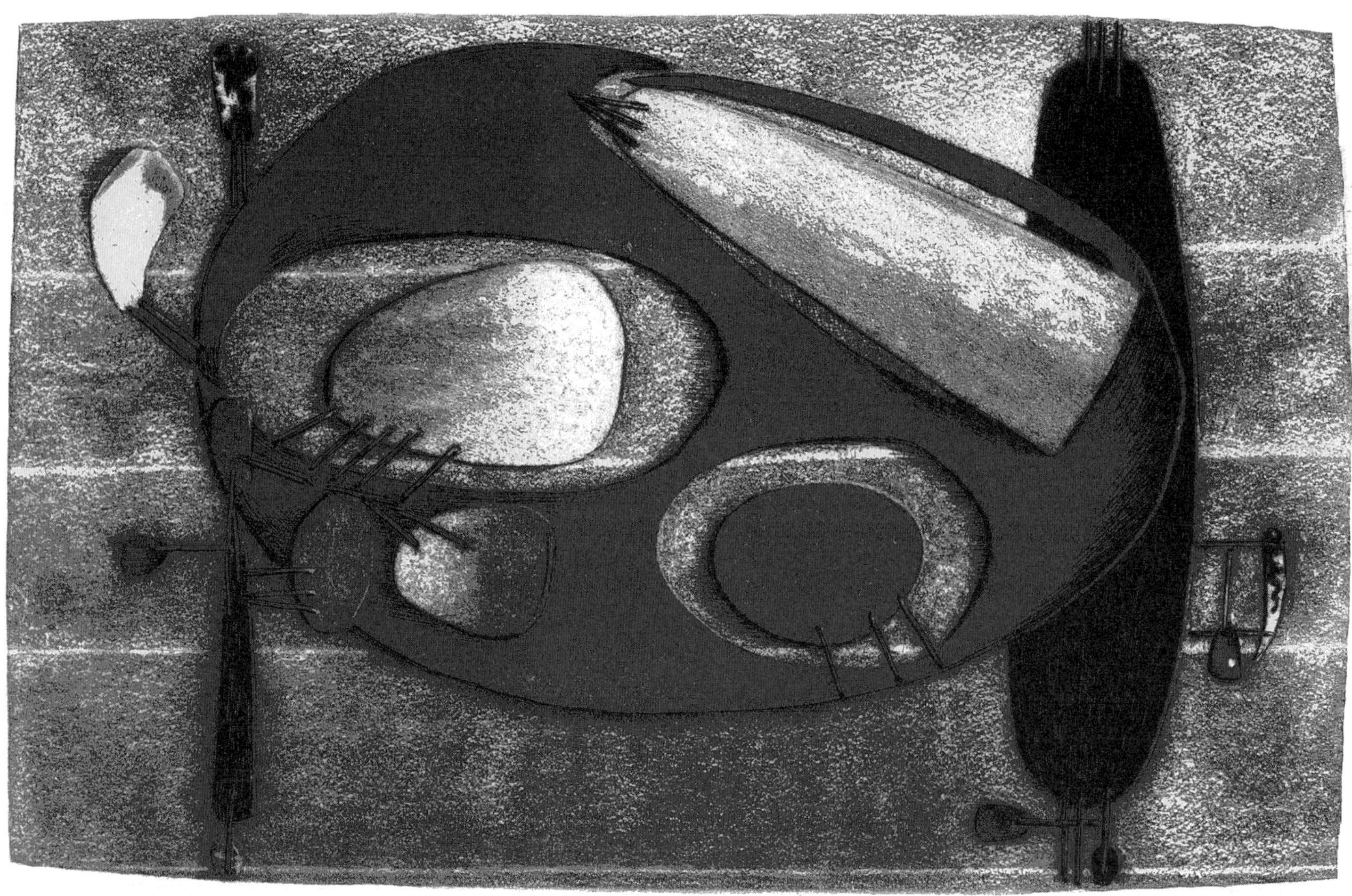

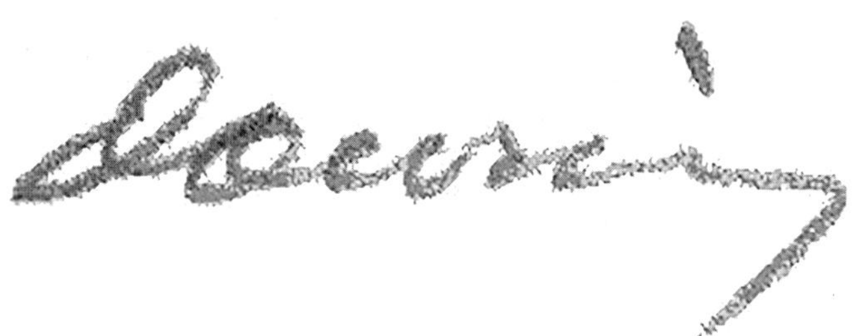

JOSEPH DUDLEY DOWNING, a member of a prominent Western Kentucky family, became internationally celebrated in the 1950s and '60s for his creation of the "stapleage," abstract collages of office supplies. Downing's fame landed him a place in Herta Wescher's history of the art form, *Collage*, published by Abrams in 1968.

Downing (1925-2007) was born in Tompkinsville and raised in Horse Cave. He served in Europe during World War II, came home and studied art at Western Kentucky University in Bowling Green. The encouragement of legendary artist-teacher Ivan Wilson was crucial to his career.

Downing was persuaded to take up optometry as a career, and he graduated from an optometry school in Chicago, Illinois. However, the creative people in his social circle there induced him to take classes at the School of the Art Institute of Chicago. By 1950 his mind was made up, and he hied himself to Paris to pursue his muse.

Only two years later he was having a one-man exhibition in the French capital, a show that confirmed him in his decision. A fellow artist named Pablo Picasso attended the display and pronounced it "well done." Downing became one of only three Americans to have exhibited in the Louvre.

His first significant American one-man exhibition came in 1962 at the Louisville Art Center. He had already had 10 such shows in Europe. Other Art Center exhibitions followed, and in 1965 Downing showed two-sided collages of painted strips of leather on wood. He also painted on roof tiles, antique barn doors, animal bones – and canvas. He worked in etching and lithography.

Downing's works are in the Paris Museum of Modern Art, the Smithsonian American Art Museum in Washington, D.C. (a stapelage), the Museum of Modern Art in New York City, the Speed Art Museum in Louisville and the Owensboro (Kentucky) Museum of Fine Art. A museum dedicated to Downing is just outside Bowling Green.

Whale Talk Number V
etching and aquatint
edition 98/125
1964
4 7/8 x 7 3/4 inches

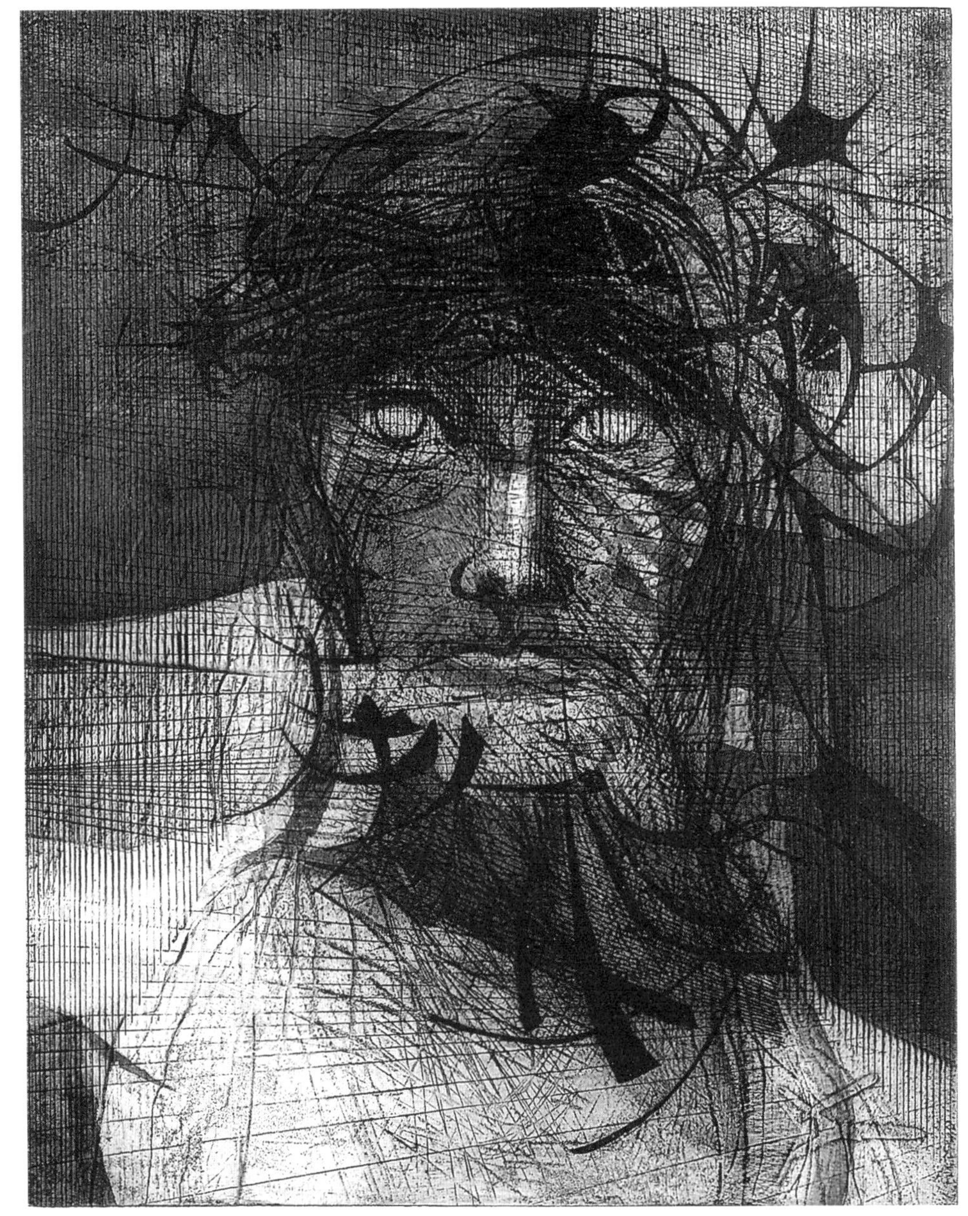

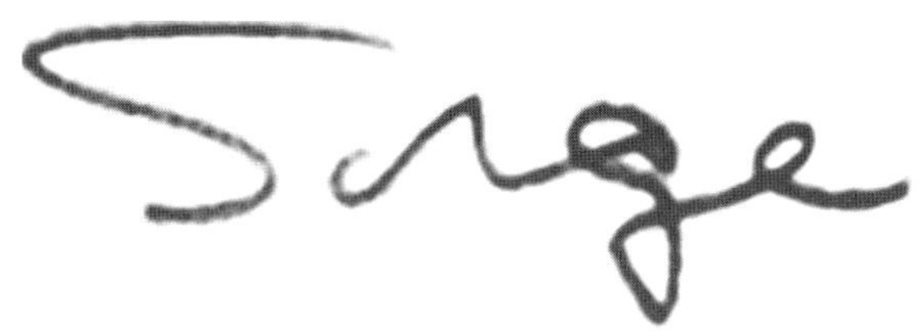

Canadian native **WALTER SORGE** (b. 1931) came to Louisville in 1964 to run the art department at the two-year-old Kentucky Southern College on Shelbyville Road.

Sorge's classes attracted area artists, including an aged Norman Kohlhepp, and influenced the local art scene, especially in printmaking. Sorge holds a master's degree from the University of California, Los Angeles, and a doctorate from Columbia University. He worked with printmaker Stanley William Hayter at the fabled Atelier 17 in Paris, France.

His first exhibition in Louisville, in 1964, comprised 30 paintings, drawings and etchings with religious and mythological themes. That same year three of his paintings were accepted into the *Mid-States Art Exhibition* at the Evansville (Indiana) Museum of Arts, History and Science. Shows followed at Bellarmine University, the Arts Club and other Louisville venues, including the Speed Art Museum in 1968. He has had at least 16 one-man shows.

Kentucky Southern College failed in 1969 and was absorbed by the University of Louisville. Sorge went to Hardin-Simmons University in Abilene, Texas, to head its art department and the next year moved on to chair the art department at Eastern Illinois University in Charleston.

After Sorge left Louisville, he continued to participate in local exhibitions, including a one-man show at the Speed in 1979, a retrospective at Stairways in 1981 and several shows in the 1990s. He also served on art juries and spoke to various arts organizations.

Sorge retired after 28 years of teaching and returned to Louisville in 2000, setting up a studio in Jeffersontown. He had a 2003 watercolor show at the University of Louisville Hite Art Institute and a 2007 show at the Jewish Community Center.

His work is in the collection of the Victoria & Albert Museum in London, England, the National Gallery of Canada in Ottawa, the Evansville museum, the Speed and the Hite.

Head of Christ
etching and aquatint
edition 13/30
19 1/2 x 15 1/2 inches

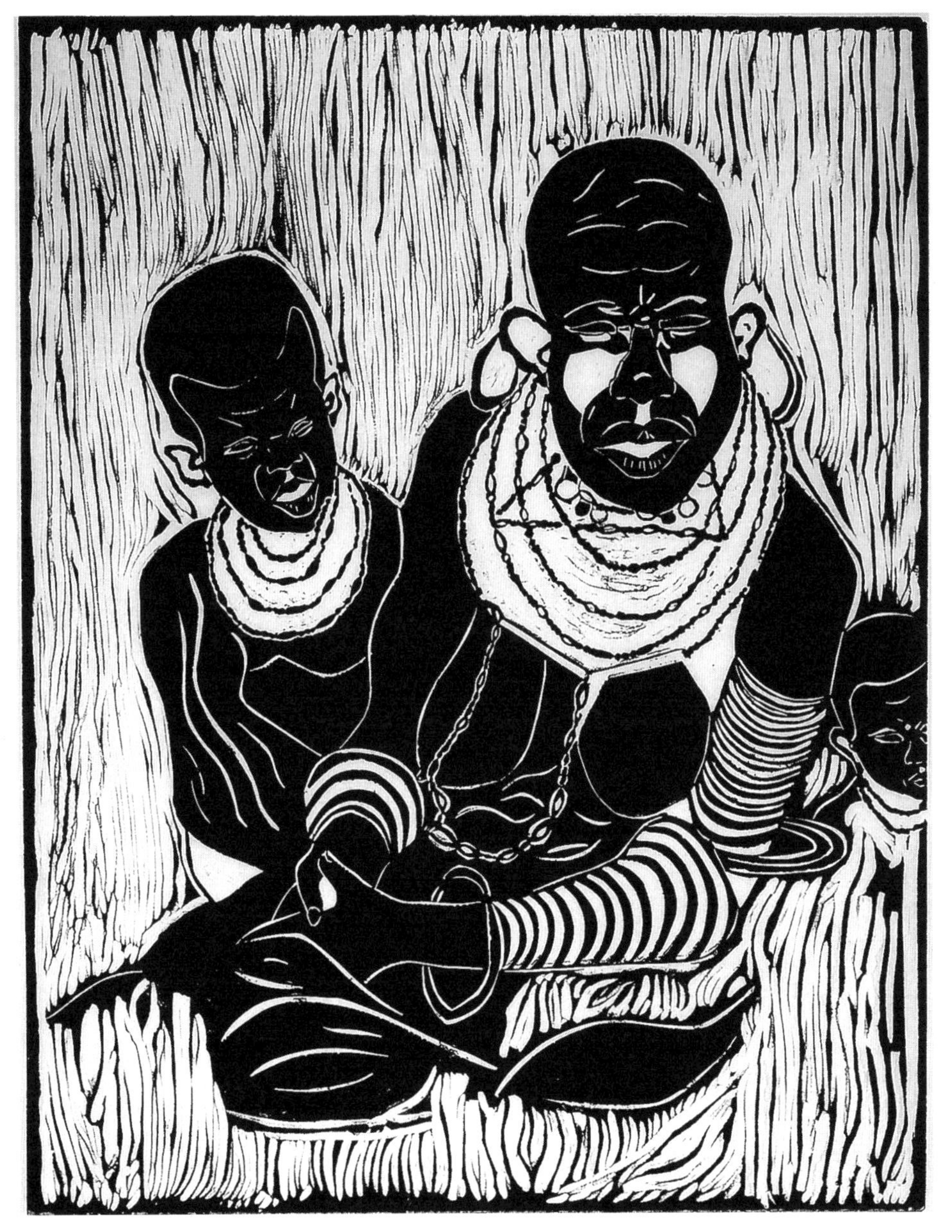

Clifford H. Morton II

In 1979 two complementary exhibitions promoted the work of area black artists, one in Louisville, one in Frankfort, Kentucky. The Louisville show, *Kentuckiana Black Art,* featured such artists as Sam Gilliam, Ed Hamilton, G.C. Coxe and Anna Huddleston. The Frankfort show, *Black Kentucky Artists,* featured the work of **CLIFFORD MOTEN HARRISON MORTON II**.

Morton (1954-2004) came from a family of Louisville and Paducah, Kentucky, educators. He was a graduate of Paducah Tilghman High School and held degrees from Paducah Community College and Kentucky State University. Morton showed in several exhibitions and received a number of honors including a 1976 purchase award from Kentucky State, the Commonwealth's historically black university.

The 1979 Frankfort exhibition was covered by the *Courier-Journal* newspaper, and Morton was photographed standing beside one of his prints. That Kentucky Arts Commission show was designed to travel the state and in 1980 came to Morton's hometown of Paducah. Morton told the *Paducah Sun* newspaper that he had been influenced by Cubist and Surrealist artists.

He taught art in the Franklin County, Kentucky, schools.

Woman and Child
block print
24 x 19 inches

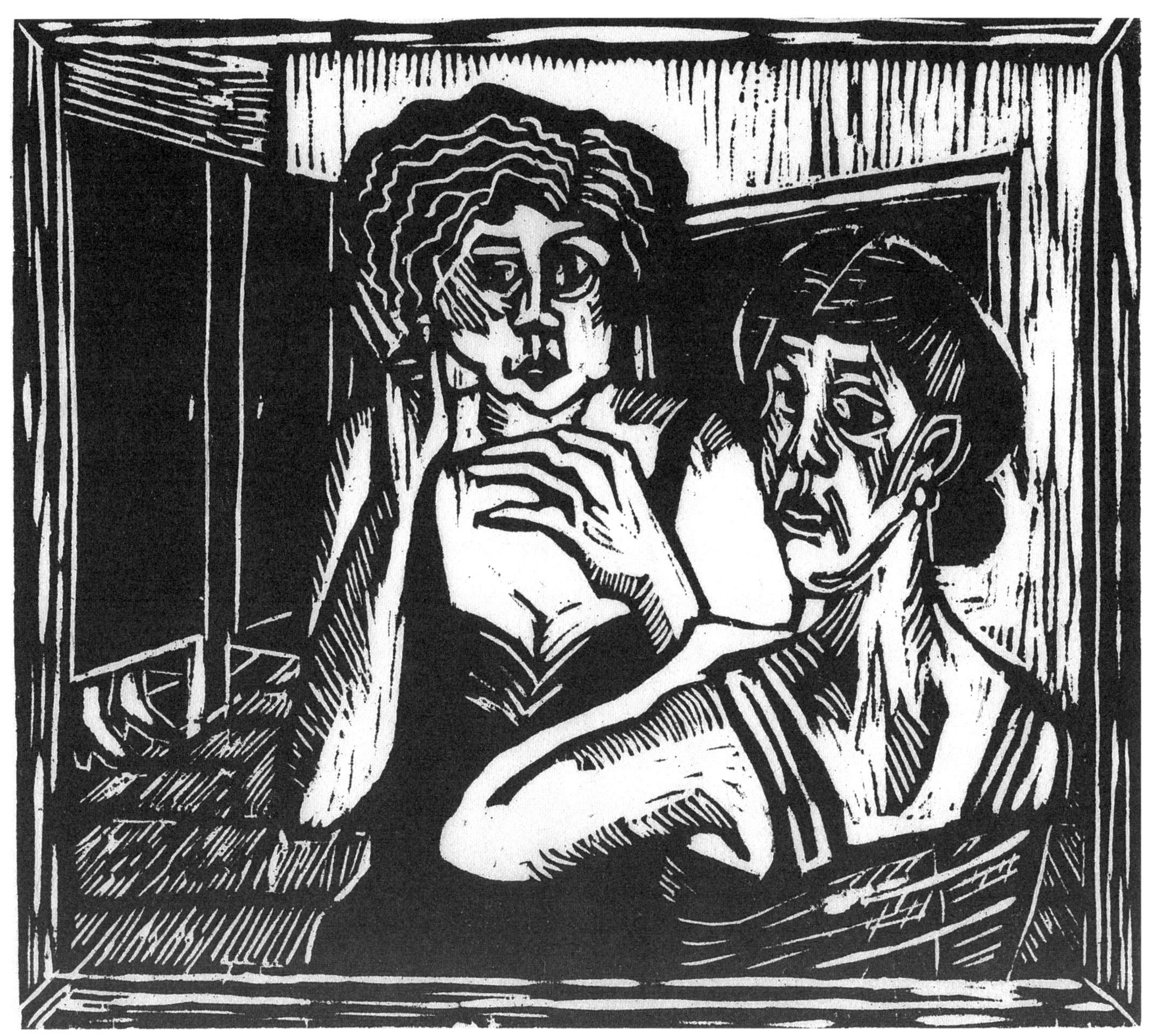

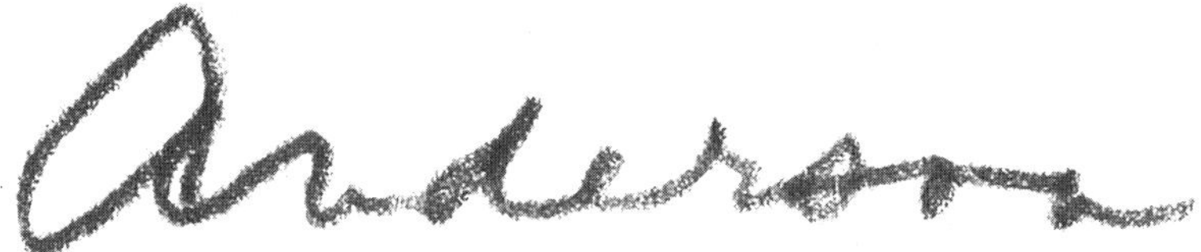

ANN STEWART ANDERSON (1935-2019) was a celebrated Louisville, Kentucky, artist known for her exploration of what it is to be a woman in today's world.

She was born in Franklin, Kentucky, and raised in Louisville. She was an art history graduate of Wellesley College in Wellesley, Massachusetts. She lived in Washington, D.C., while pursuing a graduate degree in painting at American University. She worked at the Corcoran Gallery of Art and, later, taught in the Montgomery County Public Schools in Maryland. Making ends meet was difficult in the nation's capital as many of the jobs she found paid little. "I must have thought I was an heiress," she was known to quip about lacking an independent income.

Her next stop was Chicago, Illinois, where she worked at the School of the Art Institute of Chicago. In 1975 she won the Mary Elvira Stevens Traveling Fellowship from Wellesley and did photography in Egypt. In 1977 she was back in Louisville and artist-in-residence at St. Francis School. She retired from teaching in 1991 and was named executive director of the Kentucky Foundation for Women. She continued to paint, make prints and create mosaics in paper and ceramics.

Once asked how long it took her to paint a painting, she replied, "All my life."

Ladies Room Mirror IV
block print
edition 10/10
1989
9 7/8 x 11 1/4 inches

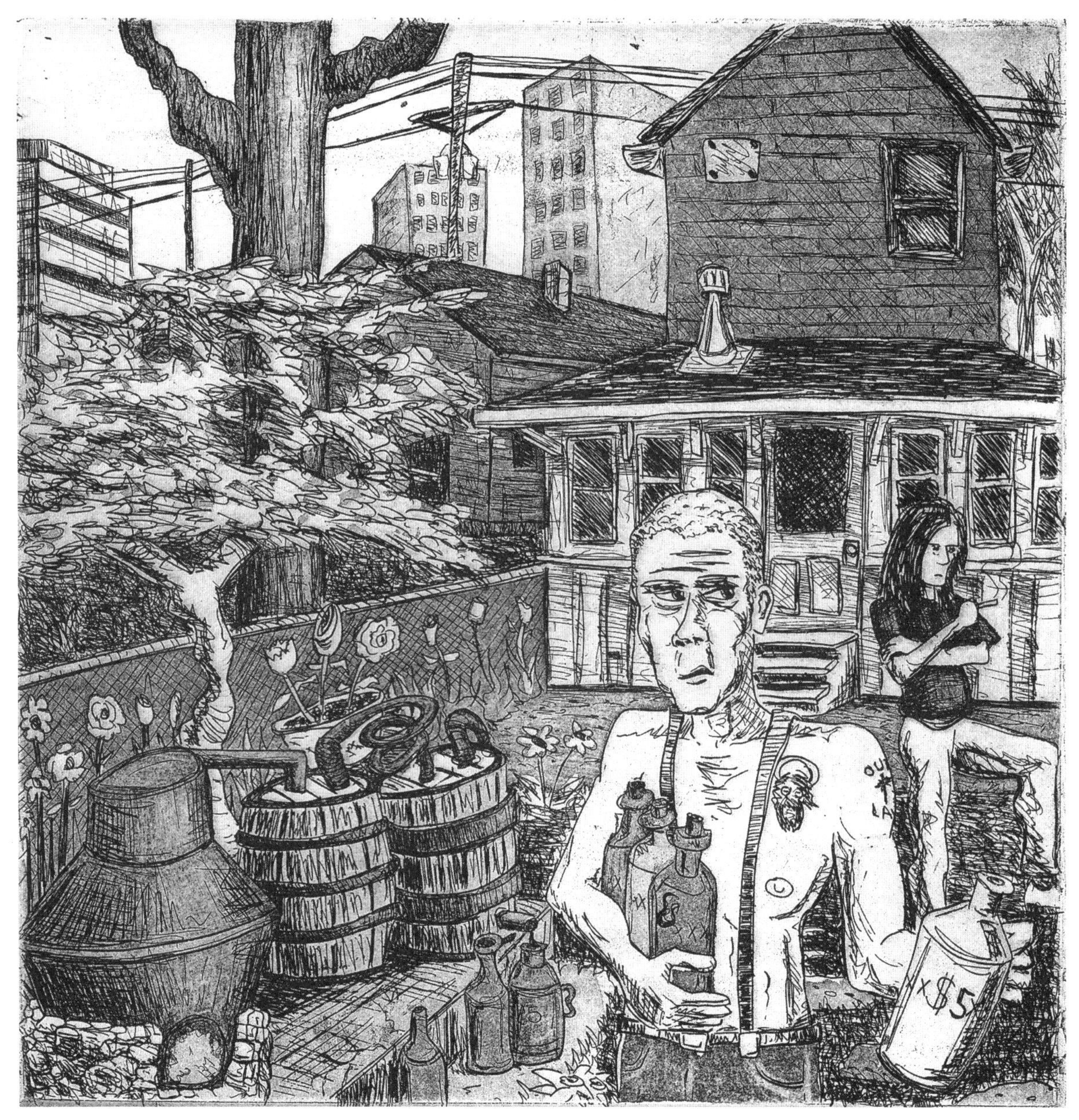
x$5

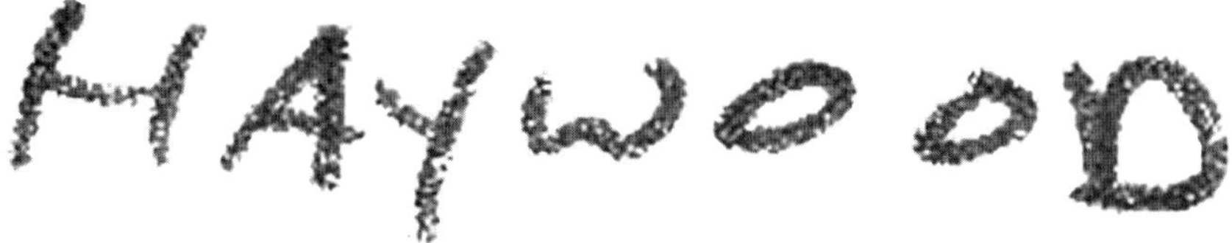

Painter, printmaker, tattoo artist and musician **JOHN WEZLEY HAYWOOD** was born in Prestonsburg, Kentucky, in 1977. Art and music played an important role in his life from an early age.

He was graduated from Morehead State University and came to Louisville to study painting at the University of Louisville and get his master's degree. He told the *Humans of Central Appalachia* website that the freedom he found in graduate school helped him develop his art "into something that was uniquely me," though "there were people there that I thought existed just to get naked in front of people."

Haywood had a studio on Mellwood Avenue in Louisville, did art shows and played music gigs. In 2004 he started tattooing, learning with "Big Daddy" Tray Benham in Radcliff, Kentucky, near Fort Knox. Feeling homesick, he returned to Eastern Kentucky and eventually opened his own tattoo shop, the Parlor Room, in Whitesburg. He plays the banjo, specializing in country, old-time mountain and bluegrass music.

Haywood has shown his art from the Appalachian Artisan Center in Hindman to the KMAC Museum in Louisville. He received a professional development grant from the Kentucky Arts Council, was a juried member of the Kentucky Crafted Market and represented the Commonwealth at *SouthernArtistry.org*.

Moonshine City
etching
edition 2/11
2004
7 x 7 inches

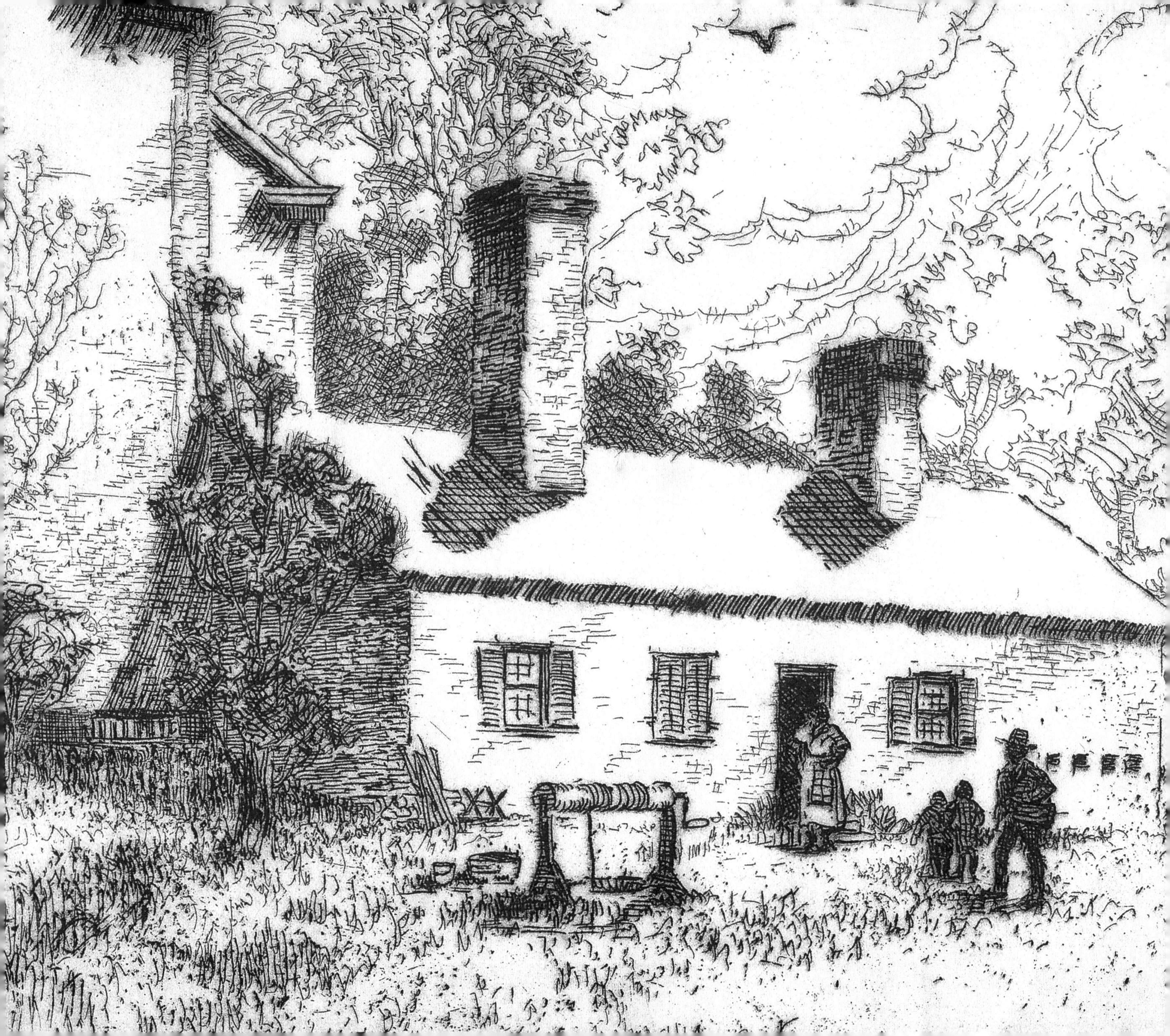

My Old Kentucky Home
(Federal Hill)

A. J. Van Leshout, *Old Kentucky Home* [detail]

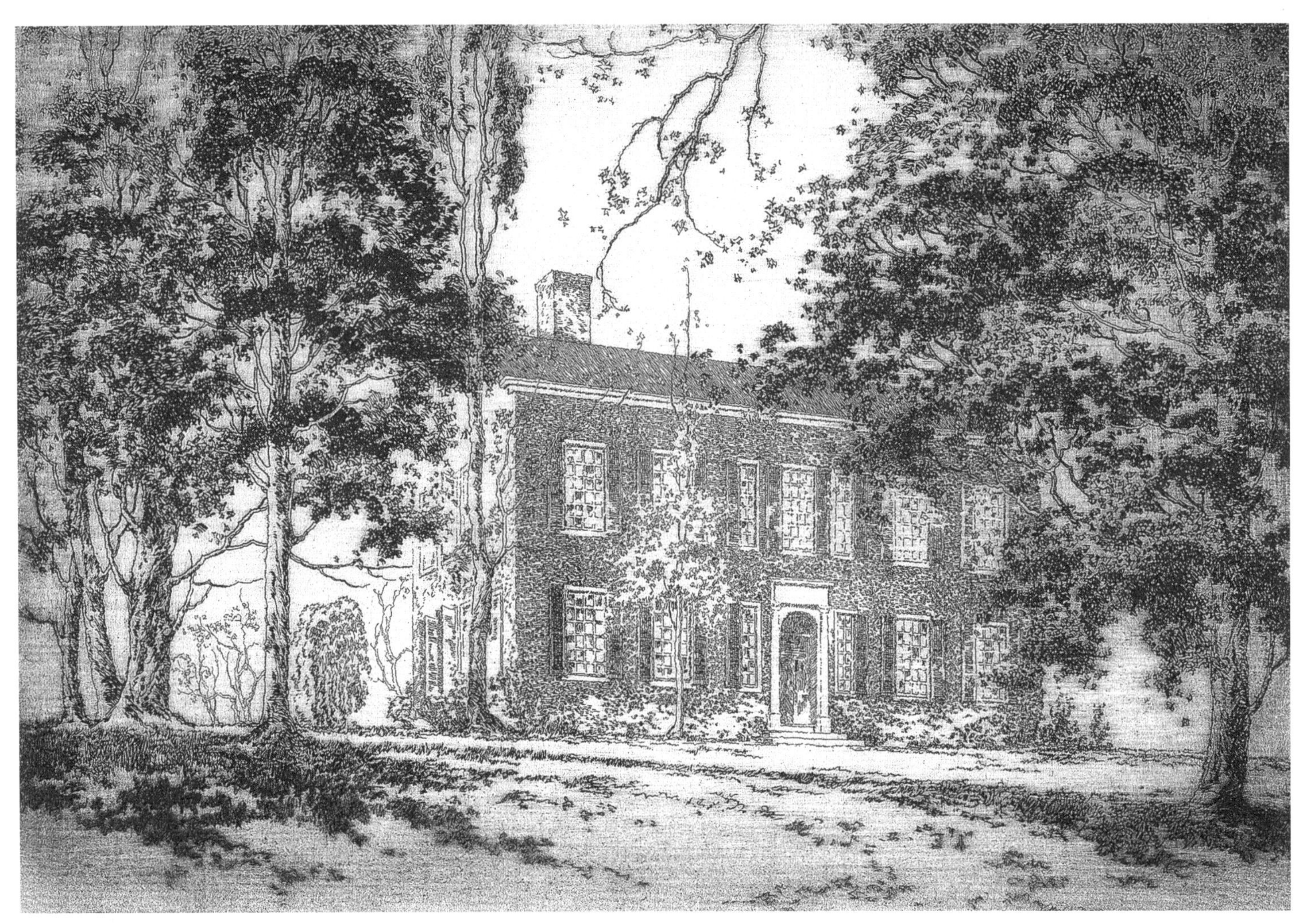

C. Winston Haberer, *Old Kentucky Home,* drypoint, 6 x 8 3/4 inches

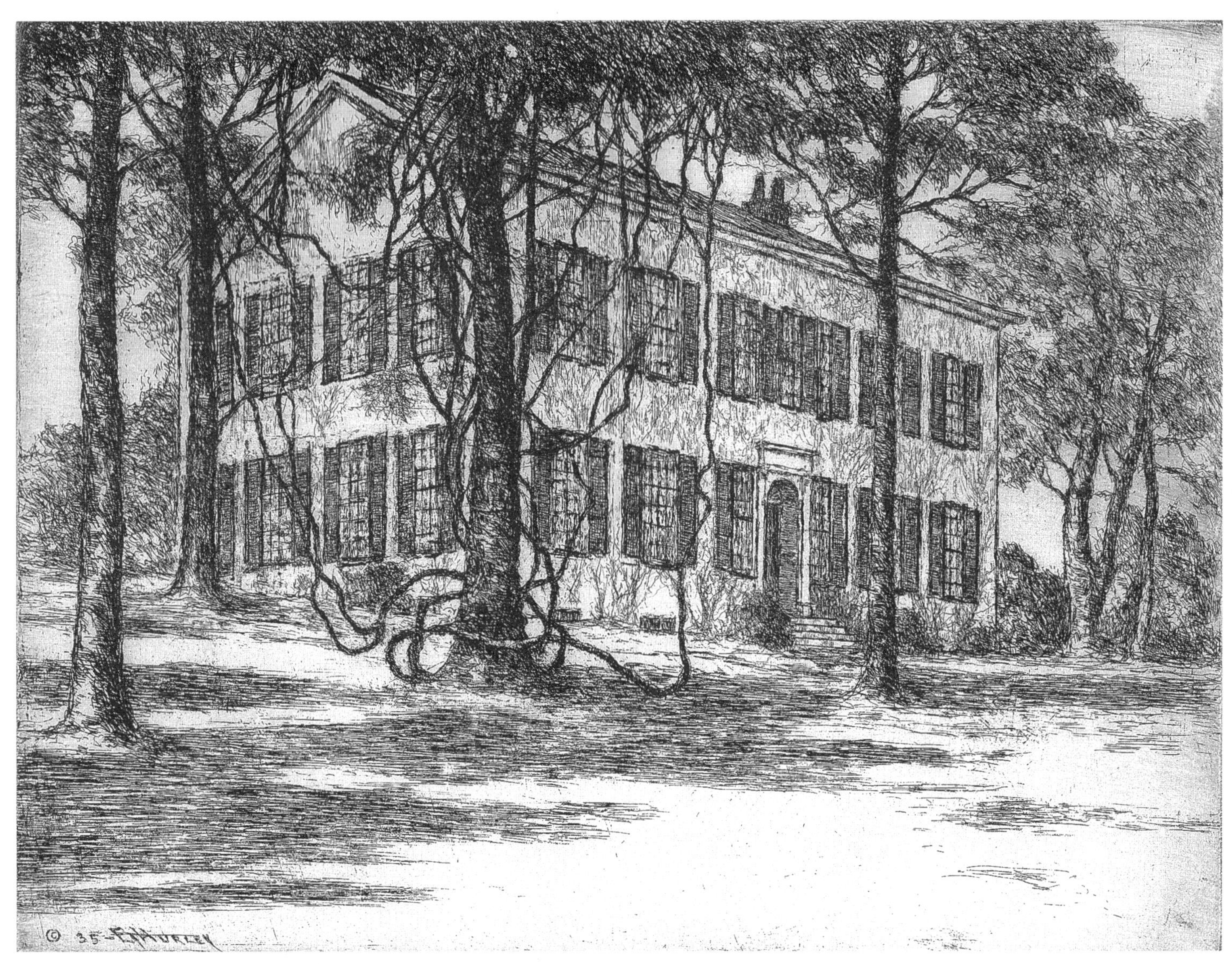

E. T. Hurley, *My Old Ky. Home - Bardstown Ky,* etching, 1935, 8 7/8 x 11 3/4 inches

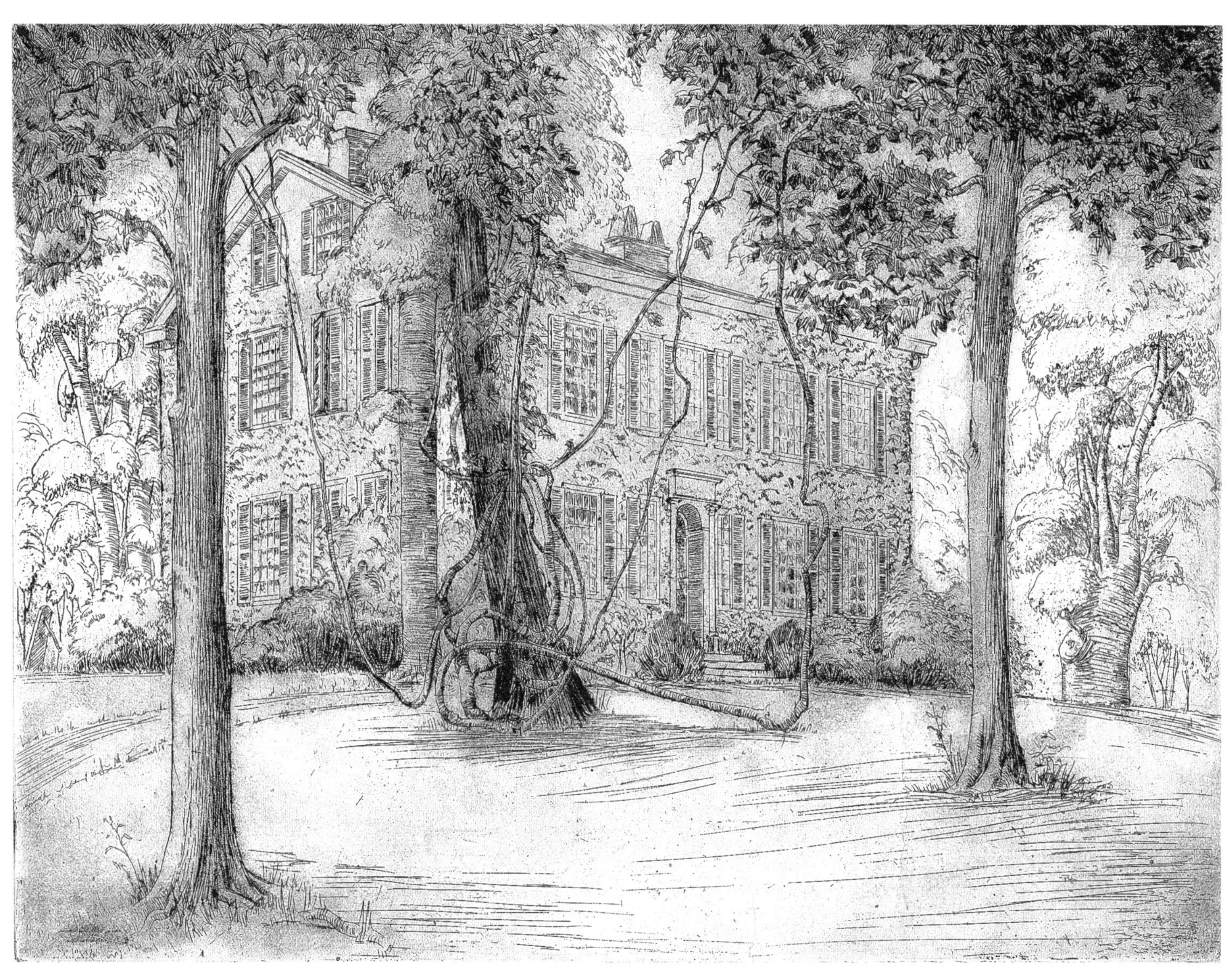

Kenneth Ozier, *The Old Kentucky Home, Bardstown, Ky,* drypoint, edition 13/16, 1935, 8 x 10 1/2 inches

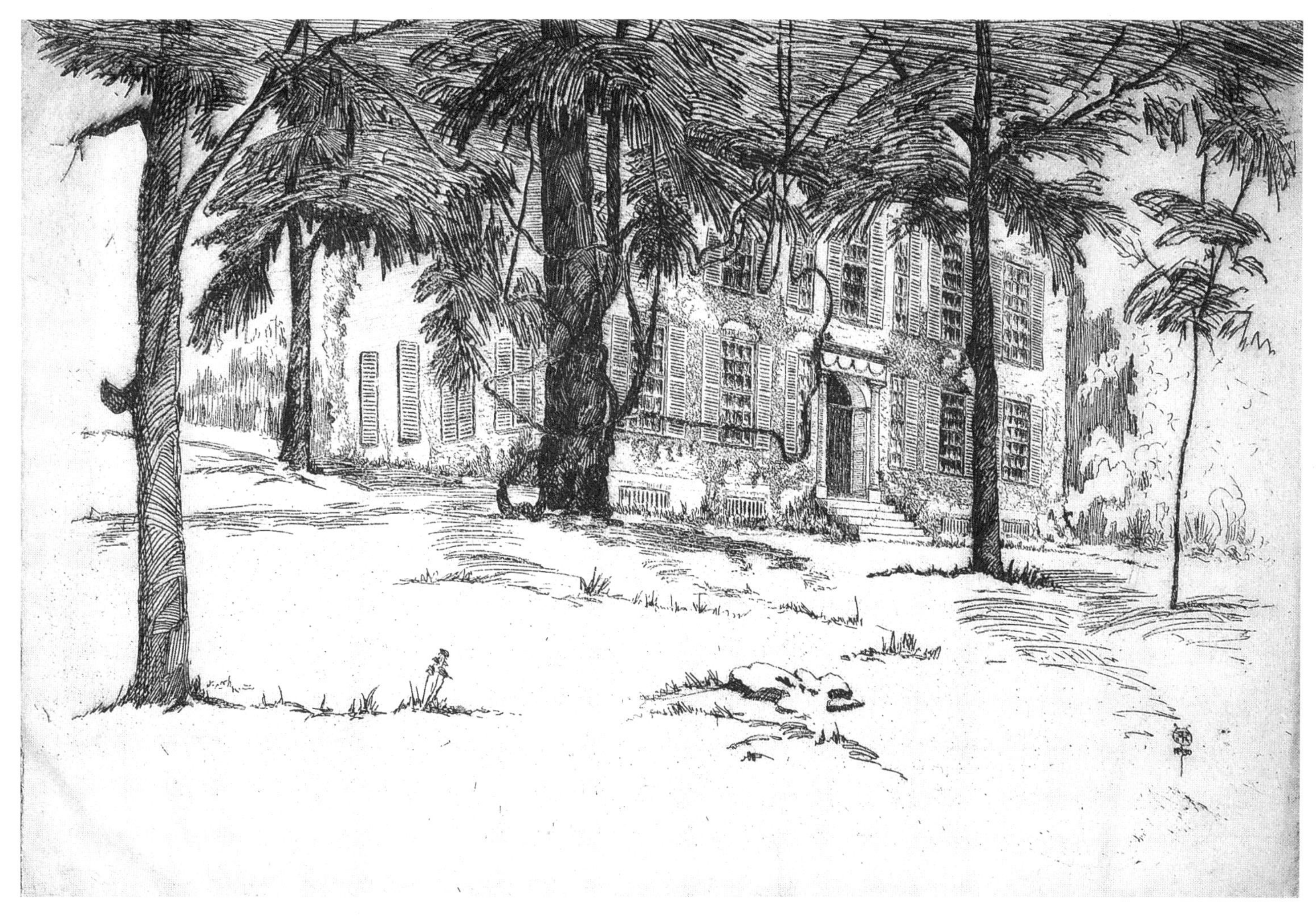

Frank Robbins, *My Old Kentucky Home*, drypoint, 1930, 5 5/8 x 8 7/8 inches

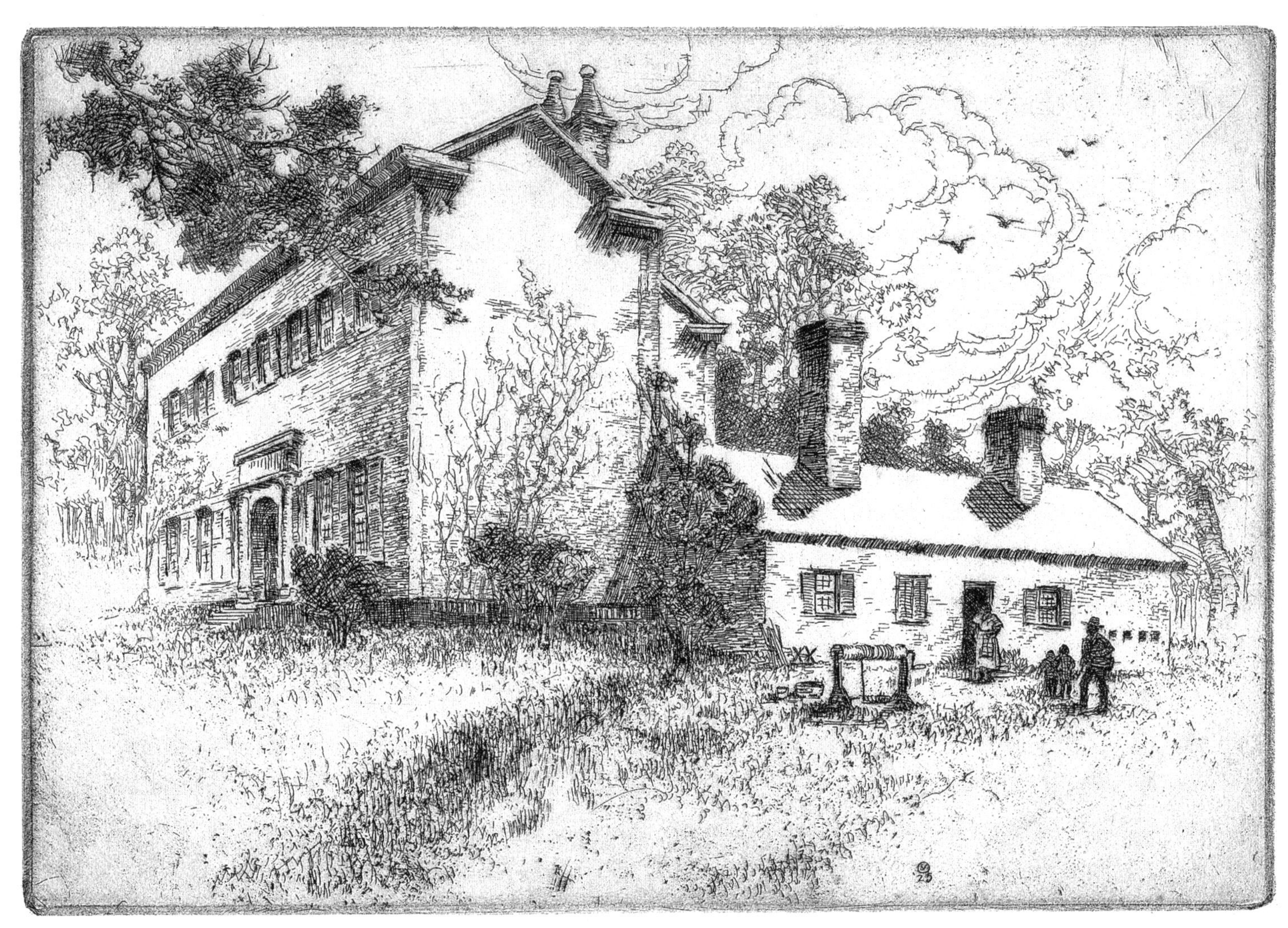

A. J. Van Leshout, *Old Kentucky Home,* drypoint, 1925, 7 1/4 x 10 3/4 inches

THE PAYNES

Warren and **Julie Payne** are private art dealers and consultants in Louisville, Kentucky. Warren is a lifelong collector of art. He was born in Harlan, Kentucky, and raised in Louisville. He holds a bachelor's degree in English from Kentucky Southern College and a master's in English from the University of Louisville. He retired from the *Courier-Journal* newspaper in 2003 after a 33-year career. Julie is also a freelance graphic designer. She was born in Oak Ridge, Tennessee, and has been a Kentucky resident since she was 10 years old. She has a B.A. in Fine Art from the University of Louisville. The couple has curated several exhibitions of forgotten regional artists and helped produce eight exhibition catalogs and three books, K*entucky: The Master Painters from the Frontier Era to the Great Depression; Clear as Mud: Early 20th Century Kentucky Art Pottery;* and *Louisville Modern: an era in art.* Julie has also recently been the curator of the Duncan Tavern Historic Center in Paris, Kentucky, the Kentucky Society of the Daughters of the American Revolution museum. The Paynes are members of the American Historical Print Collectors Society and several historical preservation and historic home organizations. Warren believes that it is important to have a sense of place and to have pride in that place. Knowing your state's art history is part of that.

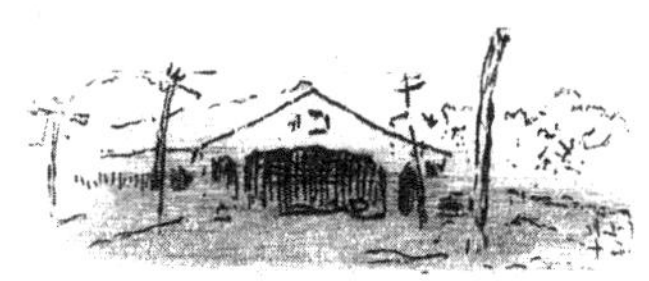

INDEX

Note: page numbers in **bold** refer to artworks.